Italian Paintings of the Sixteenth Century

THE NATIONAL GALLERY SCHOOLS OF PAINTING

Italian Paintings of the Sixteenth Century

ALLAN BRAHAM

Keeper and Deputy Director

The National Gallery, London
in association with William Collins   1985

William Collins Sons and Co Ltd
London · Glasgow · Sydney · Auckland
Toronto · Johannesburg

BRITISH LIBRARY CATALOGUING IN PUBLICATION DATA

Braham, Allan
  Italian paintings of the sixteenth century.—
  (The National Gallery schools of painting)
  1. Painting, Italian   2. Painting, Renaissance
  —Italy
  I. Title   II. Series
  759.5   ND615
ISBN 0 00 217402 2

First published 1985
© The Trustees of the National Gallery 1985

Photoset in Imprint by Ace Filmsetting Ltd, Frome
Colour reproductions by P. J. Graphics Ltd, London W3
Made and printed by Staples Printers Kettering Ltd.

The front cover shows a detail from Titian's *Bacchus and Ariadne*; the back cover Leonardo da Vinci's *The Virgin of the Rocks*.

THE NATIONAL GALLERY SCHOOLS OF PAINTING

This series, published by William Collins in association with the National Gallery, offers the general reader an illustrated guide to all the principal schools of painting represented in the Gallery. Each volume contains fifty colour plates with a commentary and short introduction by a member of the Gallery staff. The first six volumes in the series are:

Dutch Paintings by Christopher Brown
French Paintings before 1800 by Michael Wilson
Spanish and later Italian Paintings by Michael Helston
Italian Paintings of the Sixteenth Century by Allan Braham
Early Netherlandish and German Paintings by Alistair Smith
French Paintings after 1800 by Michael Wilson

Further volumes completing the series will be published this year.

Italian Paintings of the Sixteenth Century

The National Gallery's collection of Italian paintings of the sixteenth century is one of the richest in the world. The deep-rooted love of the English for the paintings of the period began in the early seventeenth century, as manifested by the collecting of Charles I and his circle, and continued in subsequent years with the acquisitions of gentlemen visiting Italy on the Grand Tour. The Italian paintings of the period continue to provide enjoyment and inspiration for the very large numbers of visitors to the National Gallery today.

Some of the greatest works of western art are illustrated and discussed in this volume: Leonardo's *The Virgin of the Rocks*,

Tintoretto's *St. George and the Dragon*, Titian's *Bacchus and Ariadne*, Veronese's *The Family of Darius before Alexander*. These are paintings that have commanded the deepest respect and admiration of posterity, establishing a standard of excellence that has left no subsequent generation untouched.

In this book the National Gallery's collection of High Renaissance paintings has been made accessible in fifty fine colour plates which are accompanied by a commentary by Allan Braham, the curator of the paintings.

ALLAN BRAHAM is the Keeper and Deputy Director of the National Gallery and in charge of the Italian paintings of the sixteenth century. He has organized exhibitions on Giovanni Battista Moroni (1978), Italian Renaissance Portraits (1979), and Spanish paintings (*El Greco to Goya*, 1981). He also writes on architectural subjects, most recently on *The Architecture of the French Enlightenment* (1980).

Introduction

Italian painting of the sixteenth century has been well represented at the National Gallery from the very earliest years. In 1824 the Government bought for the nation the collection of the wealthy financier, John Julius Angerstein, acquiring the great altarpiece by Sebastiano del Piombo of *The Raising of Lazarus* (Plate 19) and Raphael's portrait of *Pope Julius II* (Plate 9), which were the first Italian masterpieces of the period to enter the collection. Since the early years of the seventeenth century, when the appreciation and collecting of paintings first began to play a prominent part in English civilization, the great Italian artists of the High Renaissance were admired above all others, and their supremacy remained essentially unchallenged until the early years of the present century.

First of all there was Raphael, the fountain-head of the academic tradition in painting, whom Reynolds described as 'foremost of the first painters'. Though his greatest works were to be seen in Rome (fig. 1), England possessed the series of cartoons which he had made for tapestries for the Sistine Chapel. They had been bought by King Charles I in 1623, and were placed on exhibition in a special gallery at Hampton Court in the later seventeenth century. Michelangelo (fig. 2) was generally a less popular painter until the dawning of Romanticism, when the quality of *terribilità* inherent in his style was more positively welcomed. For many years, however, it was generally agreed that no painter of modern times had excelled the artists of ancient Greece and Rome, and classical sculpture (fig. 3), which had played an essential part in the development of painting in sixteenth-century Italy, was taken as evidence of the surpassing quality of the lost paintings of classical antiquity.

The English also had a particular affection for Titian and the great Venetian painters, and for the work of the famous artists of Parma, Correggio and Parmigianino. Venetian works, principally painted on canvas and generally more numerous than the panels and fresco paintings produced in Florence and Rome, were for these reasons more accessible to foreign collectors. King Charles I had in his possession over thirty paintings attributed to Titian but only two famous Raphaels, apart from the Cartoons. His collection included Correggio's *Mercury instructing Cupid before Venus* (Plate 26), and his court painter, Van Dyck, was the owner of Titian's *The Vendramin Family* (Plate 39).

At the time of the Commonwealth the several great English collections of the earlier seventeenth century were largely dis-

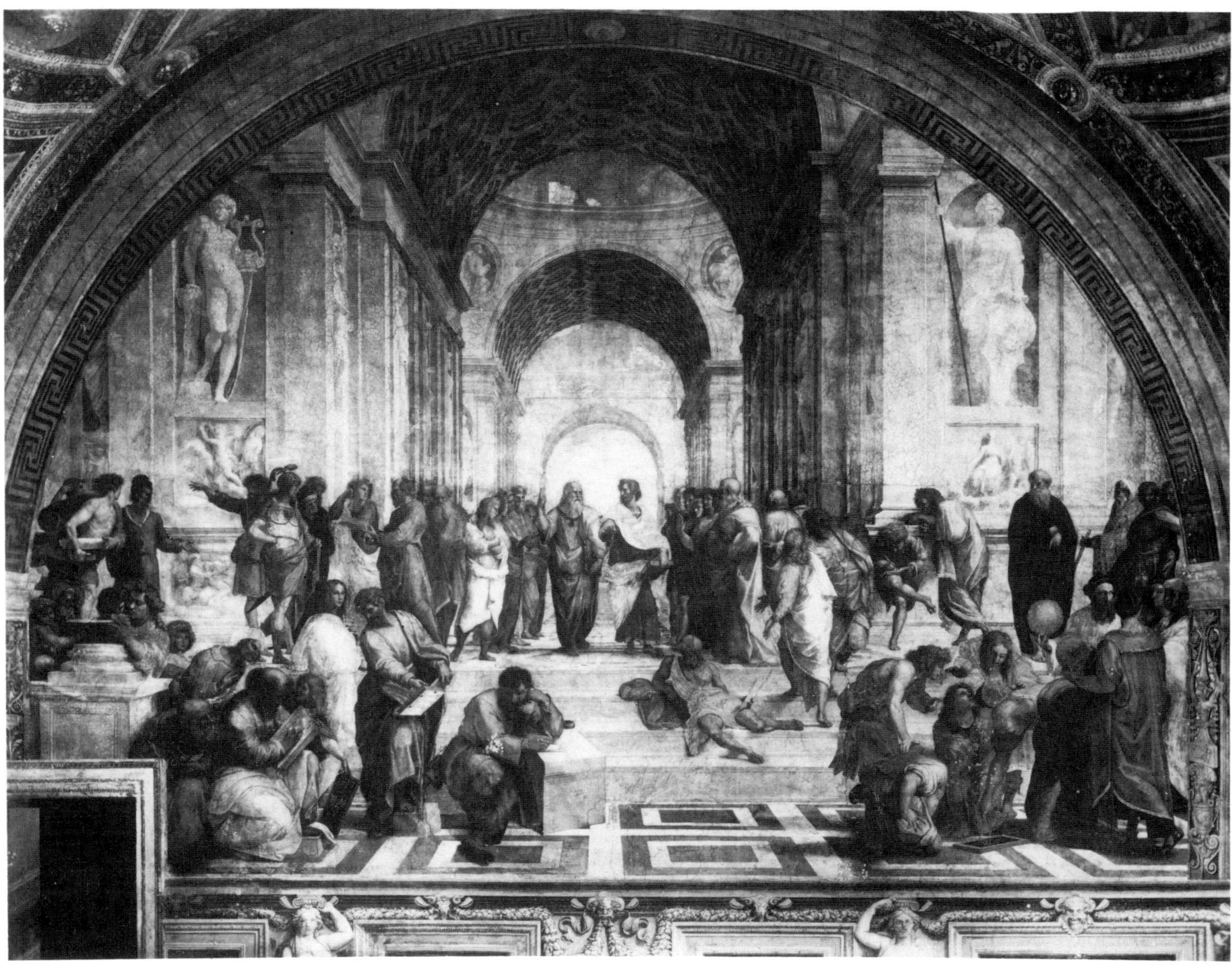

Raphael, *The School of Athens* (Rome, Vatican). From the early years of the seventeenth century for almost three centuries Raphael was the most admired of all Italian painters, especially for his frescoes in the Vatican.

persed. Charles II, however, reclaimed many of his father's paintings which had not been sold to foreign buyers, and his collection was enlarged by a gift of paintings from the Dutch Government, which comprised notable Italian works, including Bassano's *The Way to Calvary* (Plate 38). The growing interest in Italy and Italian art in the later seventeenth century is marked by the publication of the first comprehensive guide to Italy in English, by Richard Lassels (1670), and by the appearance in translation of several of Vasari's biographies of the Italian painters in a book of *Dialogues on Art* by William Aglionby (1685). Vasari had published his lives in 1550, with a second, enlarged and modified, edition appearing in 1568. He it was who first distinguished in print three epochs in the progression of painting in Italy, of which the third, and to him the finest, was initiated by Leonardo da Vinci, and dominated by

Raphael and – above all – Michelangelo. Aglionby rendered these lives into English, and – amongst their contemporaries – those of Giorgione, Titian and Andrea del Sarto.

The spread of connoisseurship as a polite accomplishment, with the Grand Tour as an essential part of the education of the rich, ensured that masterpieces of Italian painting and drawing (as well as many fakes and copies) made their way to this country in the later years of the seventeenth century and for the next hundred years. The supremacy of sixteenth-century Italian painting was persuasively maintained at the beginning of the eighteenth century in the books of Jonathan Richardson, and towards its close in the *Discourses* of Reynolds. Paintings in the National Gallery that were in English collections before the era of Napoleon included Bronzino's *Allegory* (Plate 23), which was in the Spencer collection at Althorp, Tintoretto's *S. George* (Plate 42), and two famous pictures sold to English visitors to Italy through the agency of Gavin Hamilton, a painter active in Rome in the late eighteenth century, Leonardo's *Virgin of the Rocks* (Plate 1) and *The Ansidei Madonna* by Raphael (Plates 6 and 7). A distinguished collection of mainly Florentine paintings was founded by the eccentric Lord Cowper, who lived in voluntary exile in Florence, and to him is due the importation to England of three of Pontormo's panels of the story of Joseph, paintings which were then believed to be by Andrea del Sarto (Plate 21).

The outbreak of the Revolution in France and Napoleon's domination of Europe brought about a second great influx of paintings to England, comparable with the importations of the early Stuart age. Philippe d'Orléans (Philippe 'Egalité') sold in 1792 the great collection that had been assembled mainly by his great-grandfather, the nephew of Louis XIV, and housed at the Palais Royal in Paris. Including six of the works illustrated here (Plates 12, 19, 41, 43, 47 and 48), the paintings of the Italian and French schools were finally acquired for a syndicate of British collectors, and sold in part in London in 1798. Many more masterpieces of Italian painting found their way to England following Napoleon's conquests in Italy and in Spain. The noble families of Rome were forced by taxation to part with heirlooms that had been admired in their palaces by generations of Grand Tourists, and the English were at hand to profit. The painter Alexander Day, the dealer and historian William Young Ottley, and James Irvine, acting as an agent for the dealer William Buchanan, conducted negotiations in Rome and Genoa, and their many acquisitions included Raphael's *Pope Julius II* (Plate 9) and Titian's *Bacchus and Ariadne* (Plate 15), an Aldobrandini heirloom, originally plundered from Ferrara. The Borghese collection, formed largely by Scipione Borghese, nephew of Pope Paul V, in the early years of the seventeenth century, was amongst the most vulnerable at this time and no less than six of the paintings illustrated in the following pages had been on display for many years in the palaces of that family.

A great variety of collectors profited from the importation of so many Italian paintings; though prices remained high, it was not only the richest noblemen and landowners who were able to acquire masterpieces. Angerstein, whose collection was acquired by the nation for £56,000, began collecting seriously after retirement from a career in banking and insurance. In 1831 came the bequest to the National Gallery of a wealthy clergyman, the Reverend William Holwell Carr, whose paintings included Titian's *Holy Family* (Plate 13) and Tintoretto's *S. George* (Plate 42). Samuel Rogers, who left to the nation Titian's *'Noli me tangere'* (Plate 12) in 1856, was a banker though then best-known as the author of a series of poems on Italy (1830). Early purchases by the Trustees of the National Gallery included Correggio's *Madonna of the Basket* (Plate 25), and two of the Gallery's Raphaels (Plates 5 and 8).

The supremacy of sixteenth-century Italian painters was not seriously assailed in the early years of the nineteenth century, and it was mainly to these artists that the public was more intimately introduced in the earliest monographs which began to appear in English. The lives of Michelangelo and Raphael were the subjects of books by Richard Duppa (1806 and 1816). William Coxe, the biographer of Sir Robert Walpole, wrote about Correggio and Parmigianino (1823), and Leonardo was presented to the English by John William Brown (1828). A monograph on Titian was published in 1829 by Sir Abraham Hume, and this was followed by another in 1830 by James Northcote, the pupil and biographer of Reynolds.

At the same time the traditional priorities of British taste, particularly for Italian painters of the seventeenth century, headed by the Carracci and Guido Reni (discussed by Michael Helston in an earlier volume in the present series), were being challenged by the claims of other schools and other centuries, and particularly by those of the Italian painters who had preceded Raphael. Criticism of the unadventurous purchasing policy of the early Trustees of the Gallery was one of the causes of a formal investigation of the Gallery's affairs by a Select Committee of the House of Commons, which led to the appointment in 1855 of Sir Charles Eastlake as the first Director. A painter whose own works were marked by a deep love of Venetian painting, and of Titian in particular, Eastlake purchased some of the most famous sixteenth-century Italian paintings in the collection (Plates 20, 32, 46 and 50), including the great Veronese of *The Family of Darius before Alexander*, which was bought in Venice in 1857 for what then seemed the enormous sum of £13,650. Though Eastlake is also celebrated for his acquisition of earlier Italian paintings, the High

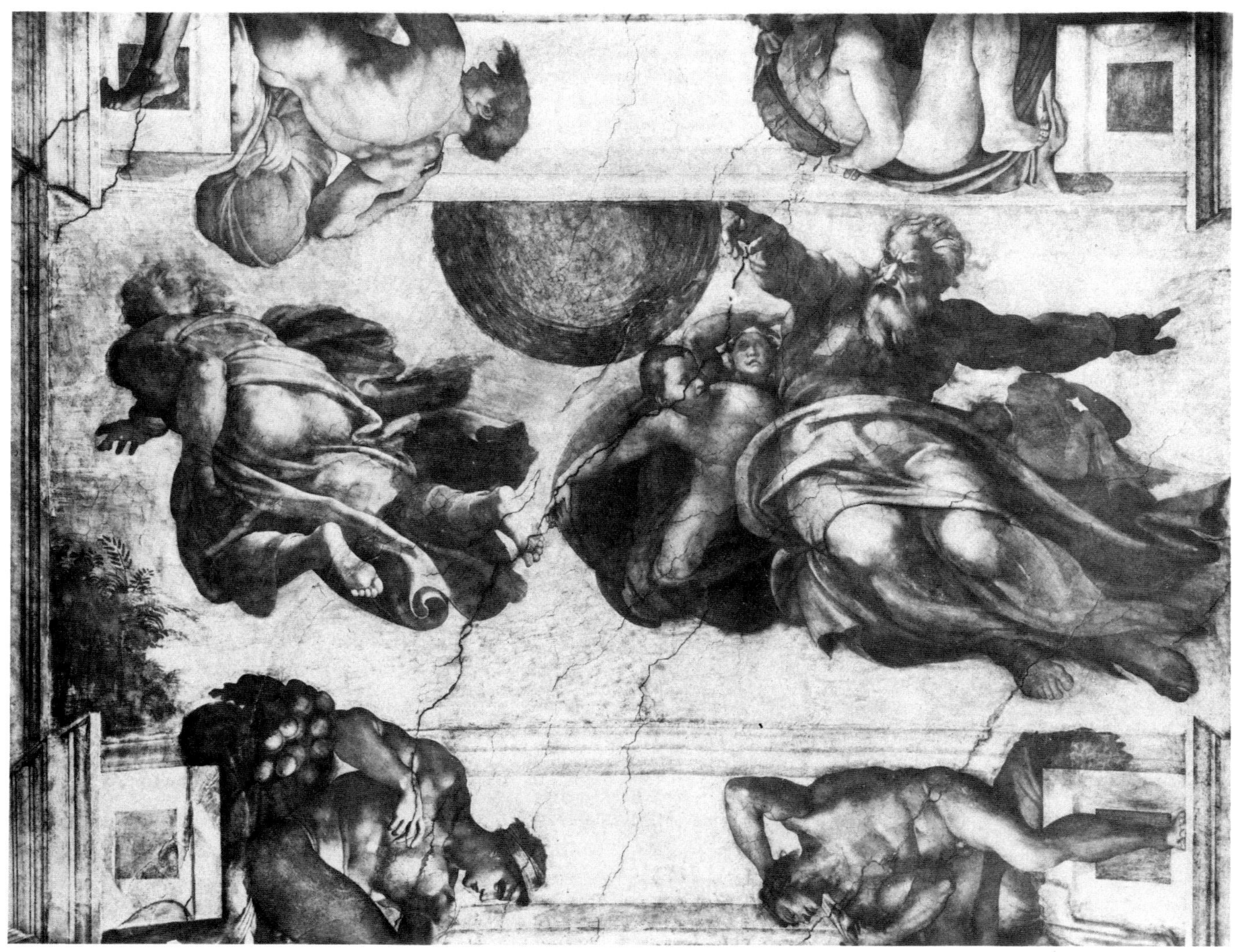

Michelangelo, *The Creation of the Sun and the Moon* (Rome, Vatican). More influential than Raphael in the sixteenth century, the art of Michelangelo declined in popularity until rediscovered by the Romantics.

Renaissance remained his favourite period, as it was also the preference of his wife, the articulate Lady Eastlake, for whom Raphael was 'the very meridian of art' (1858).

For some years after Eastlake's death in 1865 the opportunities for acquiring major paintings in Italy, and especially, after the Risorgimento, in northern Italy, continued. Eastlake's successor, Sir Frederick Burton, purchased major works there by Moretto, Savoldo and Moroni (Plates 33, 34 and 49). In the later part of the century many famous English collections were in their turn broken up and their treasures sold – paintings by Veronese and Tintoretto came from the Darnley collection, *The Virgin of the Rocks* from the country house of Lord Suffolk, and Raphael's *Ansidei Madonna* from Blenheim Palace. Opportunities to acquire Italian works of such importance have become scarcer since then, and one of the last major bequests was that of Ludwig Mond in 1924, when Dosso's *Adoration of the Kings* (Plate 37) and Titian's late *Madonna and Child* (Plate 41) were added to the collection. Amongst more recent gifts and purchases have been the Leonardo cartoon (Plate 2), presented by the National Art-Collections Fund after a large part of the considerable cost had been raised by public subscription (1962), Pontormo's panels of the story of Joseph (Plate 21), the one surviving predella panel from Raphael's *Ansidei Madonna* (Plate 7), and – most recently of all – Bassano's *The Way to Calvary* (Plate 38), purchased by private treaty in 1984.

The collection as it exists now, reflecting the priorities of four centuries of taste in England, is comparable in quality with the other schools most strongly represented in the National Gallery. Full information about the paintings and their histories is given in two of the detailed catalogues of the different schools of painting at the National Gallery, *The Earlier Italian Schools* by Martin Davies (1961), and *The Sixteenth-Century Italian Schools* by Cecil Gould (1978). The main emphasis of the Collection lies in the masterpieces of Leonardo, Raphael and the works attributed to Michelangelo, in the great Venetians, headed by Titian, and the work of other north Italian painters, Correggio, Parmigianino and, later still, in the unrivalled series of portraits by Moroni. Rather less well represented are the painters who have come to be labelled 'Mannerists' – all the various followers of Michelangelo active in Rome and Florence – though here outstanding examples of the work of Pontormo and Bronzino give a more than adequate impression of this once-neglected movement within the High Renaissance.

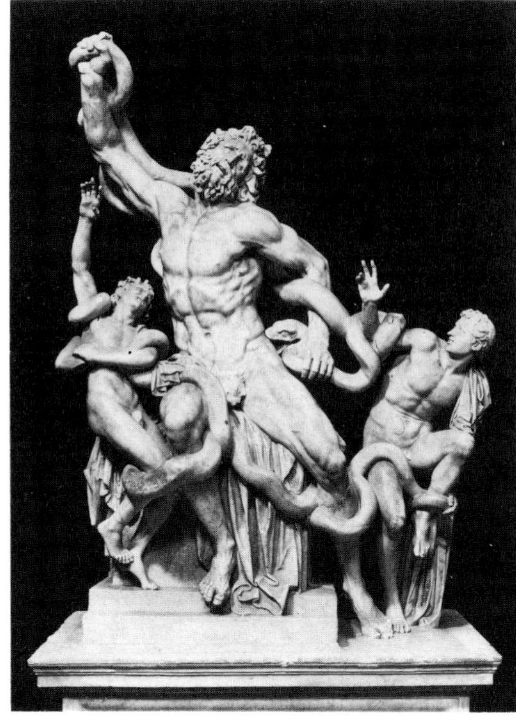

Laocoön (Rome, Vatican). Rediscovered in 1506, the *Laocoön* was one of many Hellenistic sculptures that influenced painting in the sixteenth century, and later contributed to the belief that painting in antiquity, like its sculpture, had remained unsurpassed in modern times.

Map of Italy. The country was divided in the sixteenth century into separate states, Venice ruling as far west as Bergamo, Milan dominated by Spain, and the Papal States extending north beyond the Apennines to Bologna.

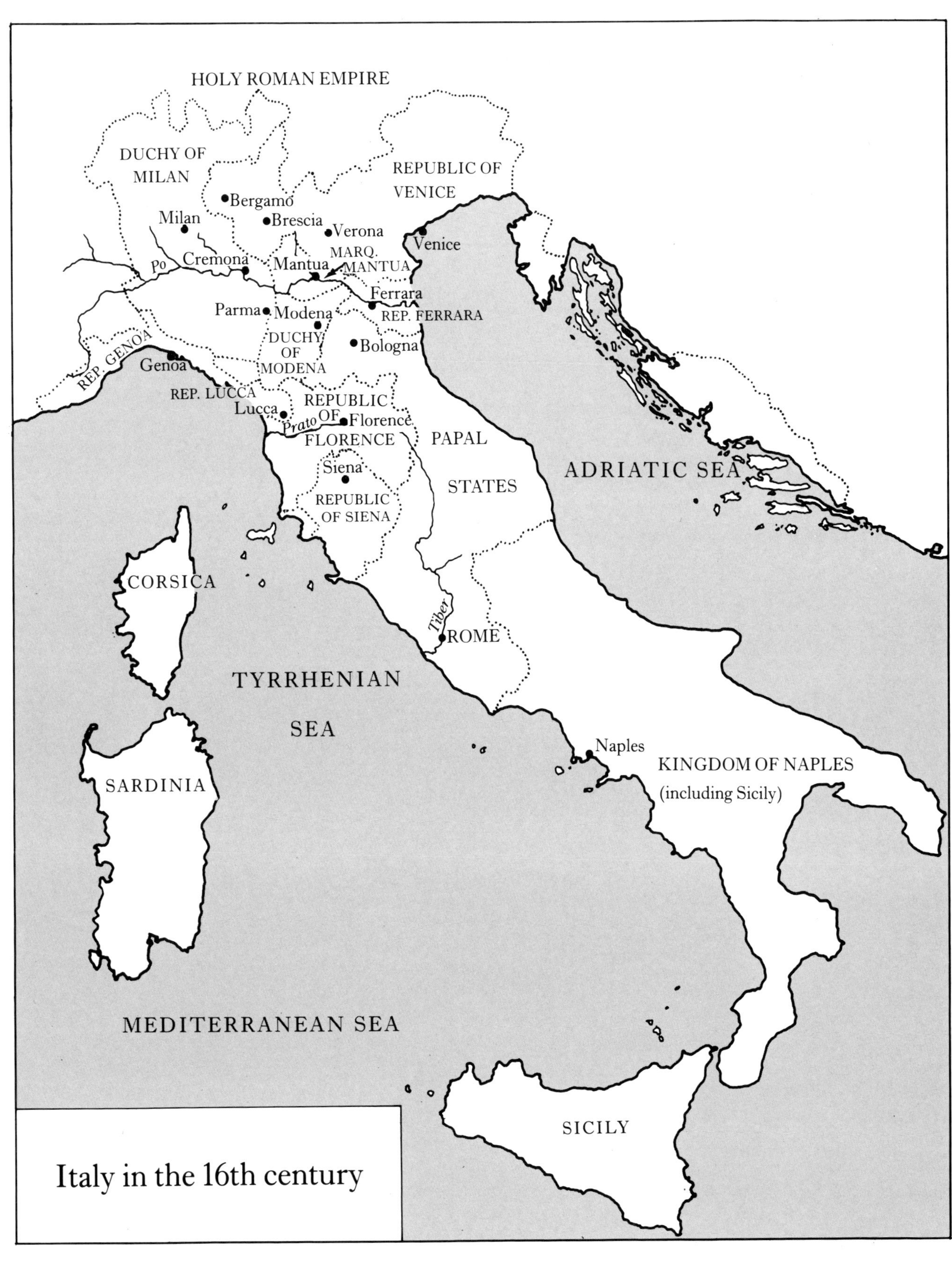

HOLY ROMAN EMPIRE
DUCHY OF MILAN
REPUBLIC OF VENICE
Bergamo
Milan
Brescia
Verona
MARQ. MANTUA
Venice
Po
Cremona
Mantua
Ferrara
Parma
Modena
REP. FERRARA
DUCHY OF MODENA
Bologna
REP. GENOA
Genoa
REP. LUCCA
Lucca
REPUBLIC OF FLORENCE
Prato
Florence
PAPAL
ADRIATIC SEA
Siena
STATES
REPUBLIC OF SIENA
CORSICA
Tiber
ROME
TYRRHENIAN
SEA
Naples
KINGDOM OF NAPLES
(including Sicily)
SARDINIA
MEDITERRANEAN SEA
SICILY
Italy in the 16th century

Leonardo da Vinci, 1452–1519

'*The Virgin of the Rocks*'
(central picture from an altarpiece) (No. 1093)

Panel, painted surface, 189.5 × 120 cm.
Purchased from the Earl of Suffolk 1880

The Virgin of the Rocks, one of the most famous of all the paintings in the National Gallery, was originally only one part of a large and elaborate altarpiece, of which the main feature was apparently a carved relief showing the Immaculate Conception of the Virgin. The altarpiece also had two panels of angels playing musical instruments, painted by Evangelista or Ambrogio Preda, which are also in the National Gallery collection (Nos. 1661–62). Leonardo and his two associates, the Preda brothers, were commissioned in 1483 to complete the altarpiece which had been ordered in 1480 for a chapel dedicated to the Immaculate Conception in the Church of S. Francesco Grande in Milan. They were to gild and colour the central relief and other parts of the altarpiece, and to provide three paintings, probably for the upper tier.

In Milan, where Leonardo had recently arrived from Florence in 1483, the world of medieval art prevailed for longer than in his native Tuscany. The great Gothic cathedral of the city was still – and for many years to come – under active construction, and altarpieces were generally far from being coherent works of art expressing, as they could in Florence, the control and the personal style of a great artist. Yet *The Virgin of the Rocks* shows how far Leonardo was supremely a man of universal genius, whose few paintings aimed to re-create the natural world with a new intensity derived from scientific observation.

Leonardo had been born near Vinci not far from Florence and trained by Verrocchio. He was already famous when he moved to Milan about the age of thirty to work for the Sforza court. After nearly twenty years he returned to Florence and came back in more troubled times to Milan where he was again active in the years 1506 to 1513. He finally left Italy in 1517 to serve King Francis I of France and died at Amboise two years later.

In the Louvre in Paris is another and earlier version of *The Virgin of the Rocks* by Leonardo, and this is probably the painting that he began in 1483 for the altarpiece in S. Francesco Grande. It may have been taken to France at a very early date, so that the painter, probably with the help of his assistants, was forced to produce a second version, which is the painting in the National Gallery.

The same cartoon (see Plate 2) may have been used for both paintings, so slight are the differences between the two. The most significant is the suppression of the hand of the angel, which lies under the shelter of the Madonna's outstretched palm in the Louvre painting, pointing across to the figure of the infant Baptist as he kneels in adoration of the

continued on p. 20

continued from p. 19

Christ Child. The composition thereby gained in mystery and inner resonance, though by the magic of Leonardo's art there was no loss of that sense the painting possesses of a heightened reality. Rocky landscapes had appeared in earlier Florentine paintings of the Holy Family, sometimes in conjunction with the theme of the Flight into Egypt, but never had there been so consistent and mysterious a cave-like setting, which mirrors the disposition of the figures and provides a terrestrial canopy for their shelter. In the distance the landscape falls away to reveal other mountains on the horizon, tinged blue in the sunlight.

Leonardo developed the study of aerial perspective, the degree of focus and gradations of colour in a distant landscape, and he had also observed the blackness of shadows, the means used to mass together the figures and the carefully described plants shadowed by the rocks in the foreground of the composition. The scientific observation of nature is thus made to serve the purposes of art, giving to the mystery of the Christian faith and to the pivotal role of the Virgin an intensity that no artist had hitherto achieved.

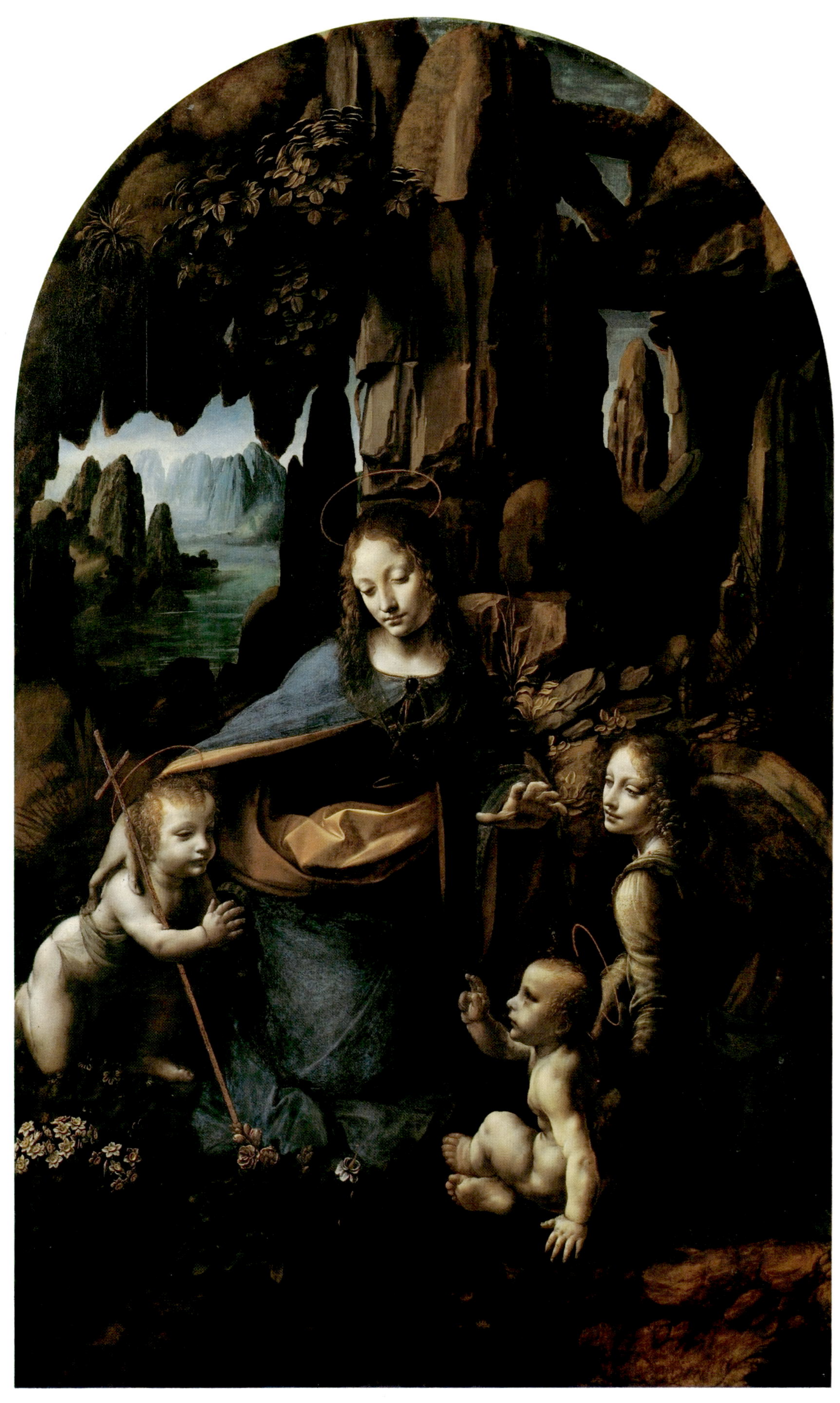

Leonardo da Vinci, 1452–1519

The Virgin and Child with S. Anne and S. John the Baptist (cartoon) (No. 6337)

Paper, 141.5 × 104.6 cm.
Presented by the National Art-Collections Fund 1962

Drawing played an important part in all branches of Leonardo's work, and most of his paintings were preceded by numerous studies on a small scale in which the artist experimented with different ways of presenting his figures in the final picture. From these sketches a full-scale 'cartoon' was made ready to be attached to the surface prepared for the paint, so that the design could be transferred, normally by punching the outlines of the composition through the paper. Leonardo would have been familiar with this technique from his early years of training in Florence, but he later developed the cartoon beyond its purely practical function so that it became sufficiently detailed to be treated as a finished work of art. Indeed, when Leonardo returned to Florence from Milan about 1500 a cartoon by him of the Virgin and Child and S. Anne was put on public display, and Vasari described the sensation it caused: 'men and women, young and old, continued for two days to flock for a sight of it to the room where it was, as if to a solemn festival, in order to gaze at the marvels of Leonardo'.

This drawing probably formed the basis for Leonardo's painting of *The Virgin and Child and S. Anne* which is now in the Louvre. The National Gallery cartoon would have marked one of the main stages towards the development of this composition, and may have been made in Milan in the later 1490s. The theme of the Christ Child blessing S. John derives from *The Virgin of the Rocks* (Plate 1), but in other ways the design shows a greater concentration and could scarcely be imagined forming part of a compartmented altarpiece.

The theme of the Virgin with her mother, S. Anne, was not a new one; it had appeared in medieval art and in paintings of the earlier Renaissance, where its formal and hieratic character was not disguised. Treated by Leonardo, the subject is made disturbingly vivid as a mystical emanation of the Christian faith. Though the forms of the figures are so softly rounded, there is no doubt of their real weight, of the limbs inhabiting the draperies. The faces, too, are described with that sensitivity to the subtleties of human expression for which Leonardo has remained for many the unsurpassed master.

With drawing as the medium, the setting of the figures could remain unspecified (a tree and distant mountains appear in the Louvre painting), and even parts of the figures are left unfinished and thus subject to further revision. The pointing hand of S. Anne, which recalls the action of the angel in the earlier (Louvre) version of *The Virgin of the Rocks*, appears mysterious and undefined as it gestures heavenwards above the hand of the Child, raised precociously to bless the Baptist and the arm stretched out to caress his cheek. The destiny of the Child and his future Baptism are miraculously revealed, and S. Anne turns, smiling gravely, towards her daughter.

When Leonardo came to revise his composition in the painting in the Louvre, S. Anne was given greater prominence, her head forming the apex of a pyramidal composition, in which the Virgin sits across her knees stretching out to the Child and smiling to him as he embraces a lamb. Though the design appears more fluent without the pointing hand and with the adult heads no longer juxtaposed in Janus-like proximity, the monumental figure of the Virgin, poignant and reflective, was thereby sacrificed and exists now only in the cartoon.

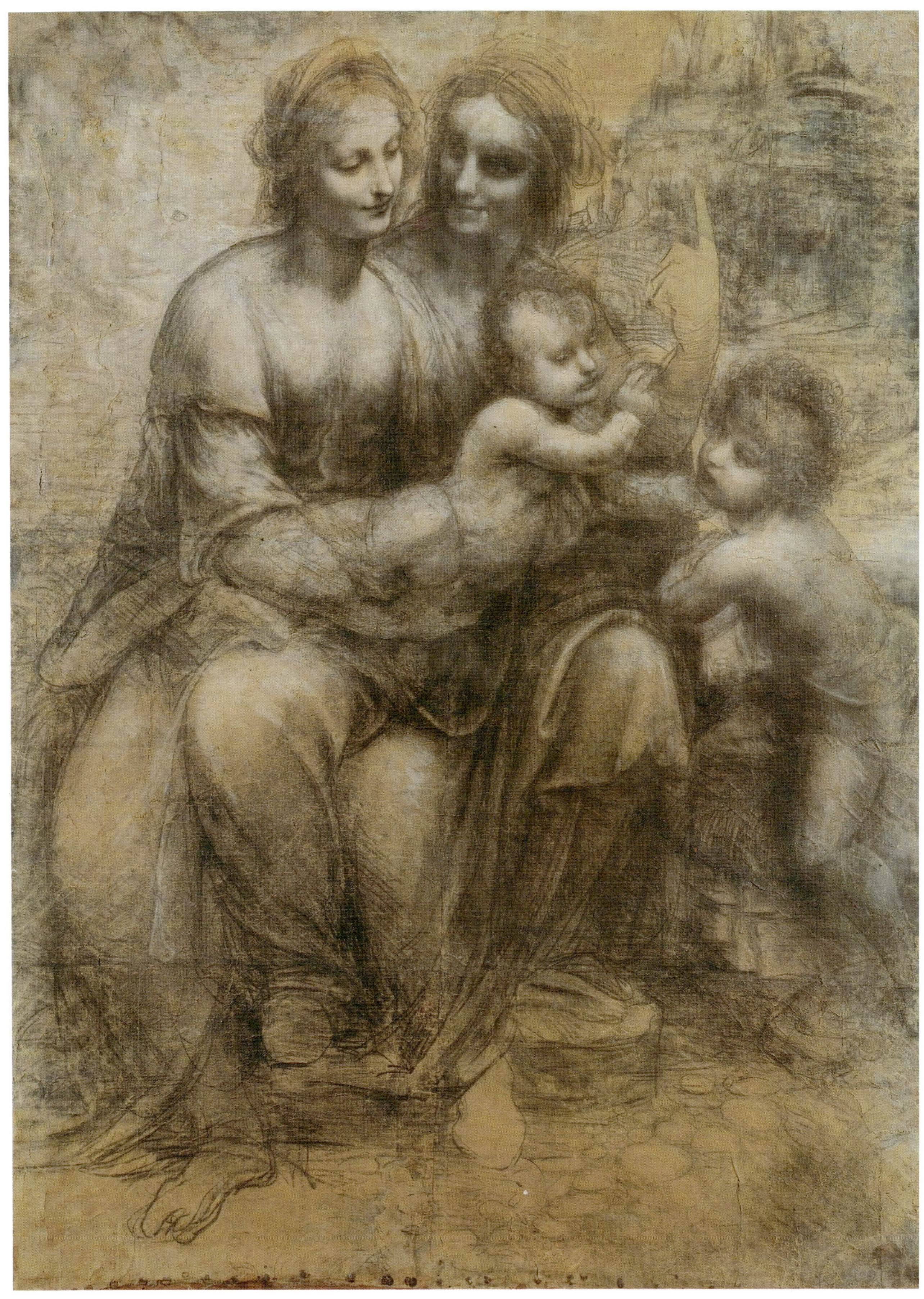

Ascribed to Michelangelo, 1475–1564

Madonna and Child with the Infant Baptist and Angels (*'The Manchester Madonna'*) (unfinished) (No. 809)

Panel, 105.4 × 76.8 cm.
Purchased 1870

Michelangelo was in his mid-twenties when Leonardo returned to Florence, and the two artists were shortly to work together on frescoes of battle scenes in the Palazzo della Signoria, unfinished and now lost paintings which are recorded in copies. Born in 1475, Michelangelo had been apprenticed to the painters Domenico and David Ghirlandaio, closely studying at the same time the work of their great Florentine predecessors, Giotto and Masaccio. His precocious talent as a sculptor was well appreciated and he had lived under the protection of the Medici, the unofficial rulers of Florence. After their expulsion in 1494, he fled to Bologna and Venice, subsequently spending five years in Rome, where his work included the famous *Pietà* in S. Peter's.

The *Madonna and Child with the Infant Baptist and Angels* is probably the earliest surviving painting by Michelangelo, and it has many of the characteristics that would be expected of his painted work in the early 1490s. It is described as a work by 'The Master of the Manchester Madonna' – so-called after the painting had been shown as a work by Michelangelo at the famous Art Treasures exhibition in Manchester in 1857 – by those who deny the attribution, but the other paintings ascribed to this same master are all markedly inferior in quality. The influence of Ghirlandaio is present in the picture – it was indeed formerly attributed to him –

and the technique is in the customary style adopted for tempera painting. The green underpainting for the flesh and the underdrawing of the draperies sketched directly on the gesso remain fully visible on the left where the panel is unfinished.

Traditional though it may be in many ways, the painting also has an experimental and carefully meditated character that suggests the hand of a young artist of genius. In style it resembles a marble relief with closely juxtaposed figures crowding the front plane. Elaborate draperies, with multiple white highlights and intensely coloured shadows, create much of the surface incident, dispersing the psychological drama of the scene.

The subject is in effect one of pathos, ambitiously – if not entirely successfully – conceived in terms of physical action. The Child and the young Baptist, who bear a marked resemblance to the children in the paintings of Masaccio, form a contrasting pair. The Child stretches out to grasp a book in the hand of the Virgin, while she looks reflectively towards the Baptist, who turns away as though meditating the future of this Child so active with future promise. The presence of the angels to the sides enlarges upon the theme, and those to the right (one of whom bears a certain resemblance to the youthful Michelangelo) serve to balance the asymmetry of the central figures.

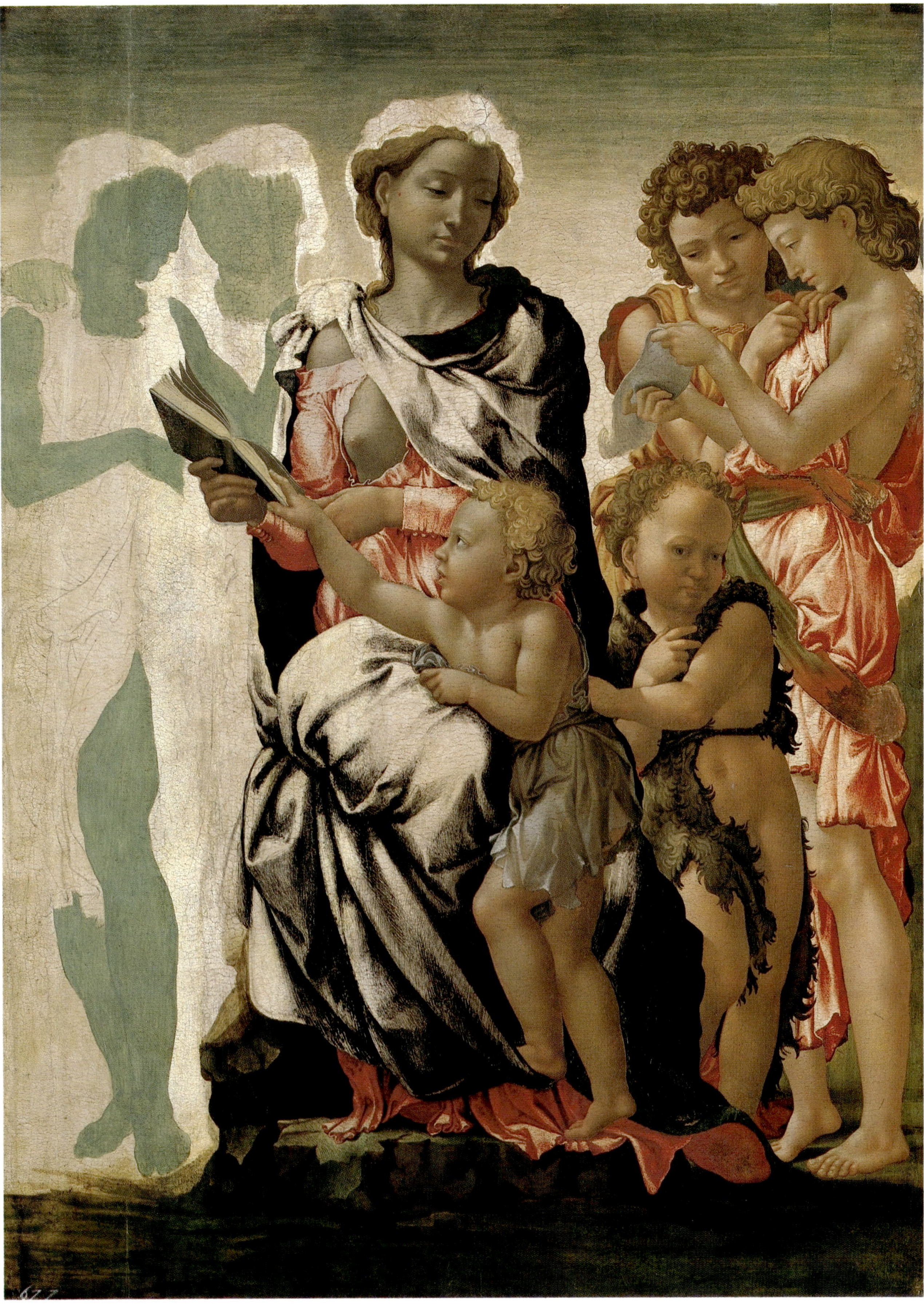

Michelangelo, 1475–1564

The Entombment (unfinished) (No. 790)

Panel, 161.7 × 149.9 cm.
Purchased 1868

Michelangelo spent the years 1501 to 1508 predominantly in Florence, though with a short visit to Rome where he was present in 1506 when the *Laocoön* (fig. 3) was unearthed. In Florence he carved the marble *David* and executed his only certain easel painting, the Doni tondo, a circular panel of the Holy Family, which is now in the Uffizi Gallery. The fresco that he was painting for a wall of the Palazzo Vecchio of the *Battle of Cascina*, as a companion to Leonardo's *Battle of Anghiari*, was left unfinished when Michelangelo was summoned to Rome by Pope Julius II to begin work on frescoing the vault of the Sistine Chapel.

The Entombment, a large, ambitious and unfinished panel, has a strong claim to being a work of this, Michelangelo's second Florentine period. The picture is notably sculptural in character, resembling not so much a relief as a three-dimensional group enclosed by secondary figures. The tomb itself is an unpainted area in the right background apparently with figures raising its slab, towards which the body of Christ is being carried up a flight of steps. Usually in representations of the Entombment, as in Raphael's famous painting of 1507 (Borghese Gallery), Christ is shown from the side lying in a shroud, and only with considerable ingenuity has the subject become a design showing the body of Christ from the front, made fully visible as an image of veneration and sacrifice.

It has been thought that knowledge of the *Laocoön* (fig. 3), a group of three struggling figures, lies behind Michelangelo's painting, which would supply a date for the picture after the statue was discovered in 1506 (it is unlikely to be much earlier), and the bands that are so conspicuous a feature of the painting indeed seem to have an almost snake-like appearance. They appear again in one of the so-called 'Captives' that Michelangelo later carved for the tomb of Julius II, while the figure of Christ after the Crucifixion was a subject to which Michelangelo later turned on several occasions, and one that he evidently found amongst the most moving of images.

In *The Entombment* the body of Christ and the figure to the left (probably S. John) are the most highly finished areas of the painting. Elsewhere parts remain mysteriously undefined, like stone that still awaits the chisel. The compact form in the right corner was probably to be the Virgin, with the Magdalen seated on the opposite side pointing towards Christ. Even the sex of the slender figure supporting Christ's body from the right is unclear; though this must presumably be a male figure, it was formerly believed to represent the Magdalen.

It was with increasing reluctance that Michelangelo undertook to produce easel paintings. He later supplied drawings for others to carry out in paint (see Plate 19), and his major works as a painter are the frescoes of the Sistine and Pauline chapels in the Vatican. Later still much of his creative energy was absorbed by architecture, which exercised his capacity as a designer and relieved him of the effort he so clearly experienced in manual creation.

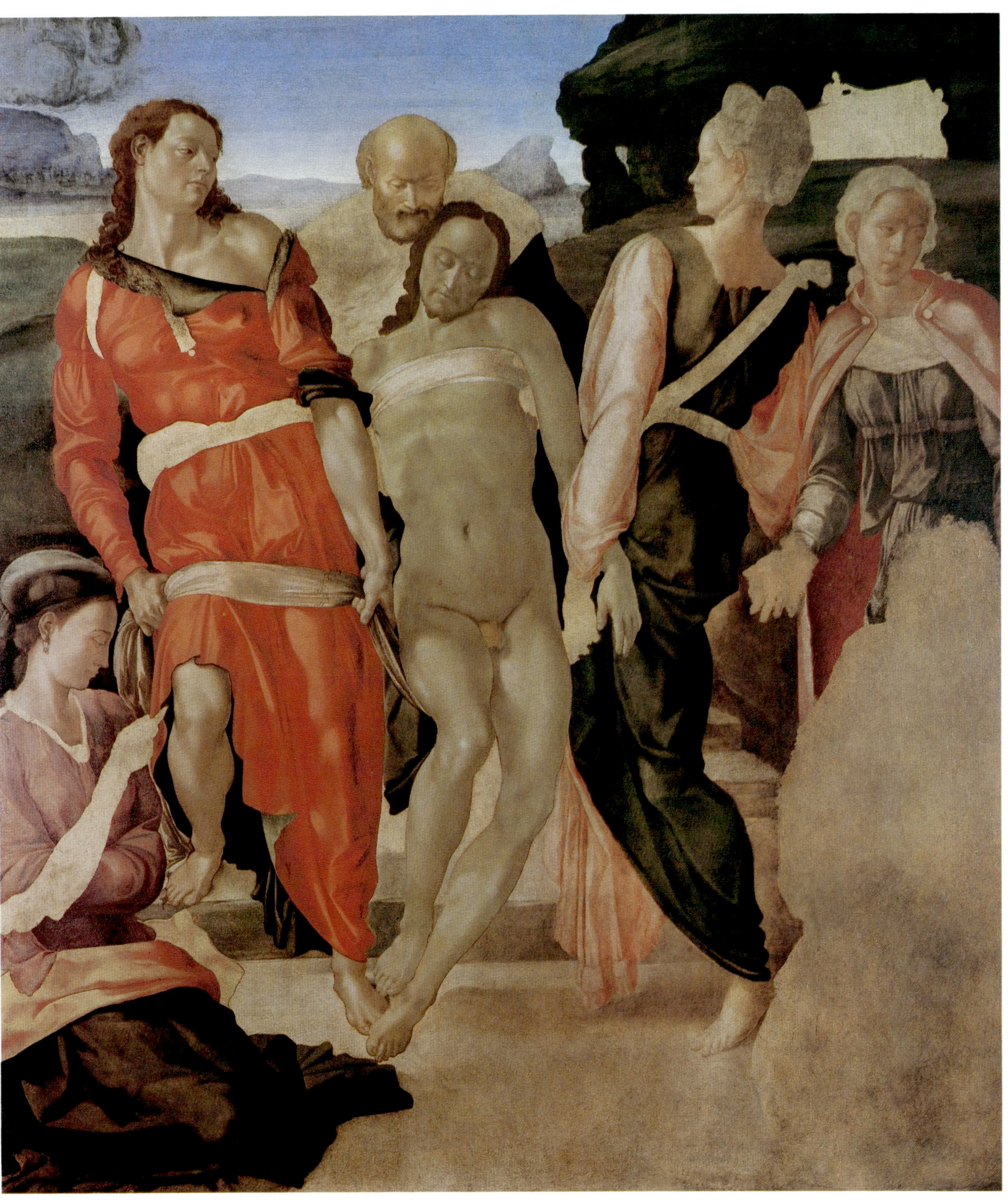

Raphael, 1483–1520

An Allegory (*'Vision of a Knight'*) (No. 213)

Panel, 17.1 × 17.1 cm.
Purchased 1847

Raphael's development as a painter was to be deeply marked by the influence of Leonardo and Michelangelo, though his was a better-adjusted temperament, and he was able to assimilate their experiments with little of the apparent difficulty that they themselves suffered as painters. Many of his earliest works combine a naïve charm that derives from early Renaissance art and a half-glimpsed promise of the changes that were later to affect his style.

Raphael was born in Urbino in 1483, the son of Giovanni Santi, a painter in the service of the Montefeltro court. Following the death of his father in 1494 Raphael was grounded in painting by one of the most famous late-fifteenth-century artists, Pietro Perugino, whose work was popular throughout central Italy, and even in Florence. Raphael's own early works were produced from 1500 onwards for several different towns in Tuscany and Umbria, and from 1504 until 1508/9, when he moved to Rome, he seems to have been mainly active in Florence.

The tiny painting known as *'Vision of a Knight'*, painted probably not long after 1500, is the secular counterpart of the lively predella panels painted by Raphael for the bases of his early altar-pieces (Plate 7) – lively both in the handling of paint and in the presentation of the subject. It is the kind of painting that can be imagined as being commissioned for a young nobleman, and it is related to a painting showing the Three Graces (now at Chantilly), which may originally have been on the back of the self-same panel.

The theme of the painting is based upon the con-flict between Virtue and Pleasure, which forms part of the legend both of Hercules and of the Roman general Scipio Africanus. The composition is divided by the trunk of a young tree, and at its base the knight lies sleeping. His head and right hand are to the left where Virtue stands, soberly clad and holding a sword and a book, which is positioned beneath a church tower on a rocky outcrop in the background. The knight's body and left hand lie to the right where the richly clad figure of Pleasure is standing, proffering flowers, before a softly undulating valley landscape. It is not clear which side the knight will choose, or whether he will thrive, like the tree, in balance between these opposing forces. The prominence of the tree even suggests that the painting may have a genealogical significance, referring to a flourishing family with origins in the classical past.

Balance is of the essence of the design, which is shown with few differences in the cartoon for the painting (also in the National Gallery), and of the treatment of the colour harmonies. The three figures are clad mainly in blue, the colour of the sky, and the most brilliant of the blues appears in the ultramarine corslet of the knight. His shield to the left is red, echoing the red of Pleasure's skirt and sleeves, and his other garments brown and green, the colours of the landscape, which also appear in the dress of Virtue and the scabbard of her sword. The charm of the painting and its chivalrous theme are rooted in the world of the earlier Renaissance, but this is given force by a capacity for design that foreshadows, not un-worthily, Raphael's later achievements in Rome.

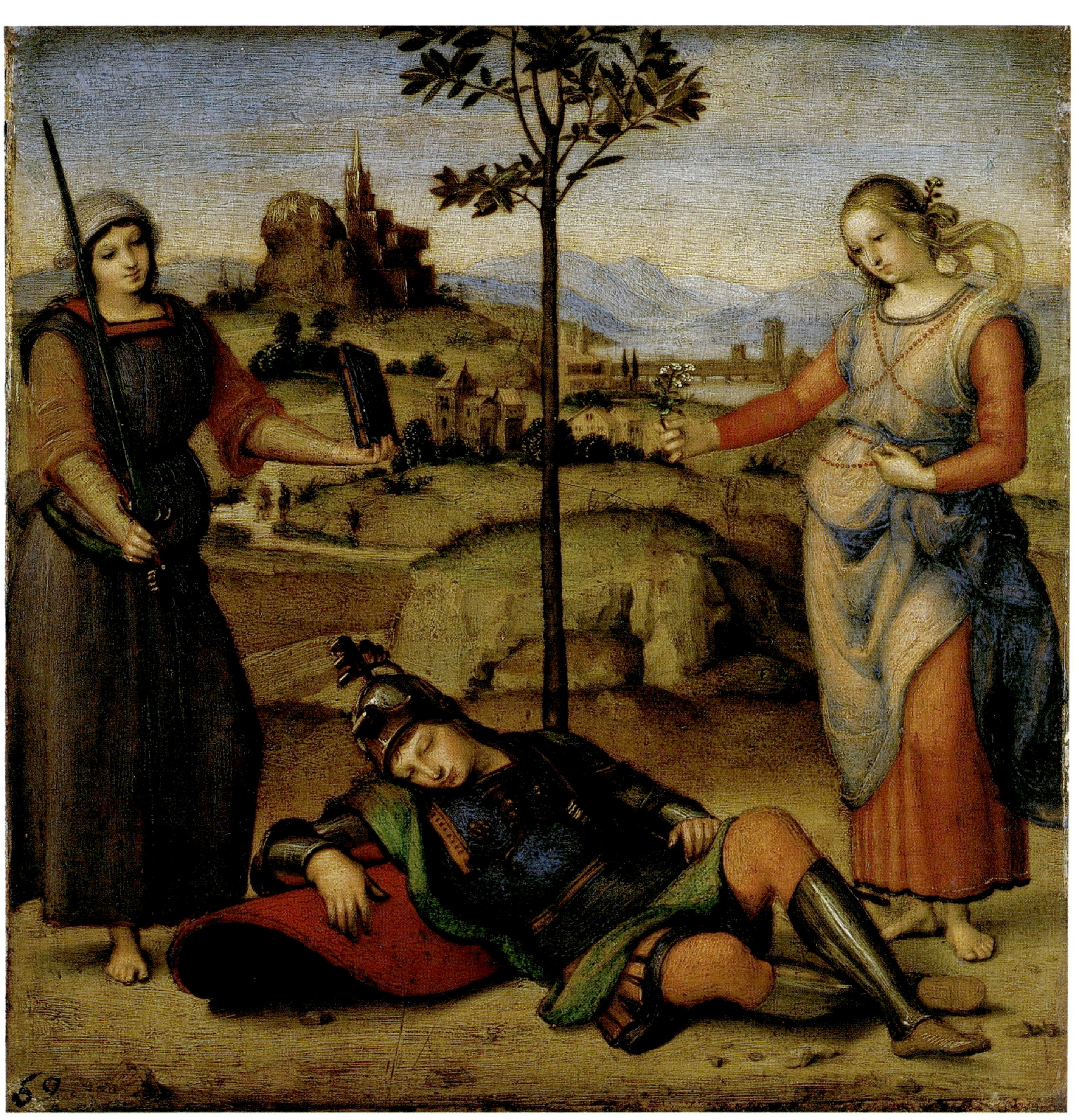

Raphael, 1483–1520

Altarpiece: Madonna and Child with the Baptist and S. Nicholas of Bari ('The Ansidei Madonna') (No. 1171)

Inscribed (on frieze above throne): .SALVE.MATER.CHRISTI.

      (on hem of Madonna's robe): MDV (?)

Panel, 209.6 × 148.6 cm.

Purchased 1885

Raphael's *Ansidei Madonna* was painted for the Ansidei family chapel in the small church of S. Fiorenzo in Perugia, and completed apparently in 1505, which seems to be the date inscribed in gold lettering on the edge of the Madonna's mantle near her left hand. The figures are shown in the setting of a vaulted room, which the painter intended to be read as an extension to the space of the real chapel, one of two shallow embrasures on the right of the nave of the church. The curved ceiling and crisply projecting cornice in the painting match the arched opening to the chapel, which was probably not greatly altered in appearance when the church was restored in the eighteenth century. The Virgin and Child faced away from the High Altar, towards the entrance to the church, and the illumination in the painting corresponds with the real lighting in the nave, which mainly derives from a high window over the east door.

This particular type of altarpiece, a *sacra conversazione*, taking place within a Renaissance church or chapel, had been developed in Florence in the early fifteenth century. Giving the illusion of near-personal intimacy with the holy beings represented on the altar, it enjoyed widespread popularity. Perugino was a capable exponent and so likewise was Piero della Francesca, who had created one of the most elaborate of such images in a late altarpiece painted for Federigo da Montefeltro, Duke of Urbino (Brera, Milan). In Raphael's altarpiece the austerity of a purely architectural setting is mitigated by the wide opening in the background, which shows a landscape that seems to overlook, from the church itself, the rolling Umbrian countryside to the south of Perugia.

In the larger and more ambitious works of his early years, Raphael appears to have relied to a considerable extent on Perugino, who is present here most obviously in the figures of the Virgin and Child, and in the elaborate vertical throne of wood on which they are raised. The two saints, John the Baptist on the left and Nicholas of Bari, to whom the Ansidei chapel was dedicated, are less closely derived from Perugino. They probably reflect Raphael's growing awareness of recent developments in Florentine art, which appears in a less linear technique and a greater amplitude in the design of the figures.

As the first major painting by Raphael to be imported to this country after the dispersal of the collection of King Charles I, the *Ansidei Madonna* occupied a special place in the history of English connoisseurship. For many years it belonged to the Dukes of Marlborough at Blenheim Palace, having been bought in Italy by Lord Robert Spencer in 1764, when travelling as a very young man on the Grand Tour. The altar had presumably been dismembered when the church was restored, and it, as well as one of the predella panels (Plate 7), had found its way to Rome and into the possession of Gavin Hamilton. Lord Robert presented the altarpiece to his brother, the 4th Duke of Marlborough, but the predella panel, which he also acquired, he retained for his own collection.

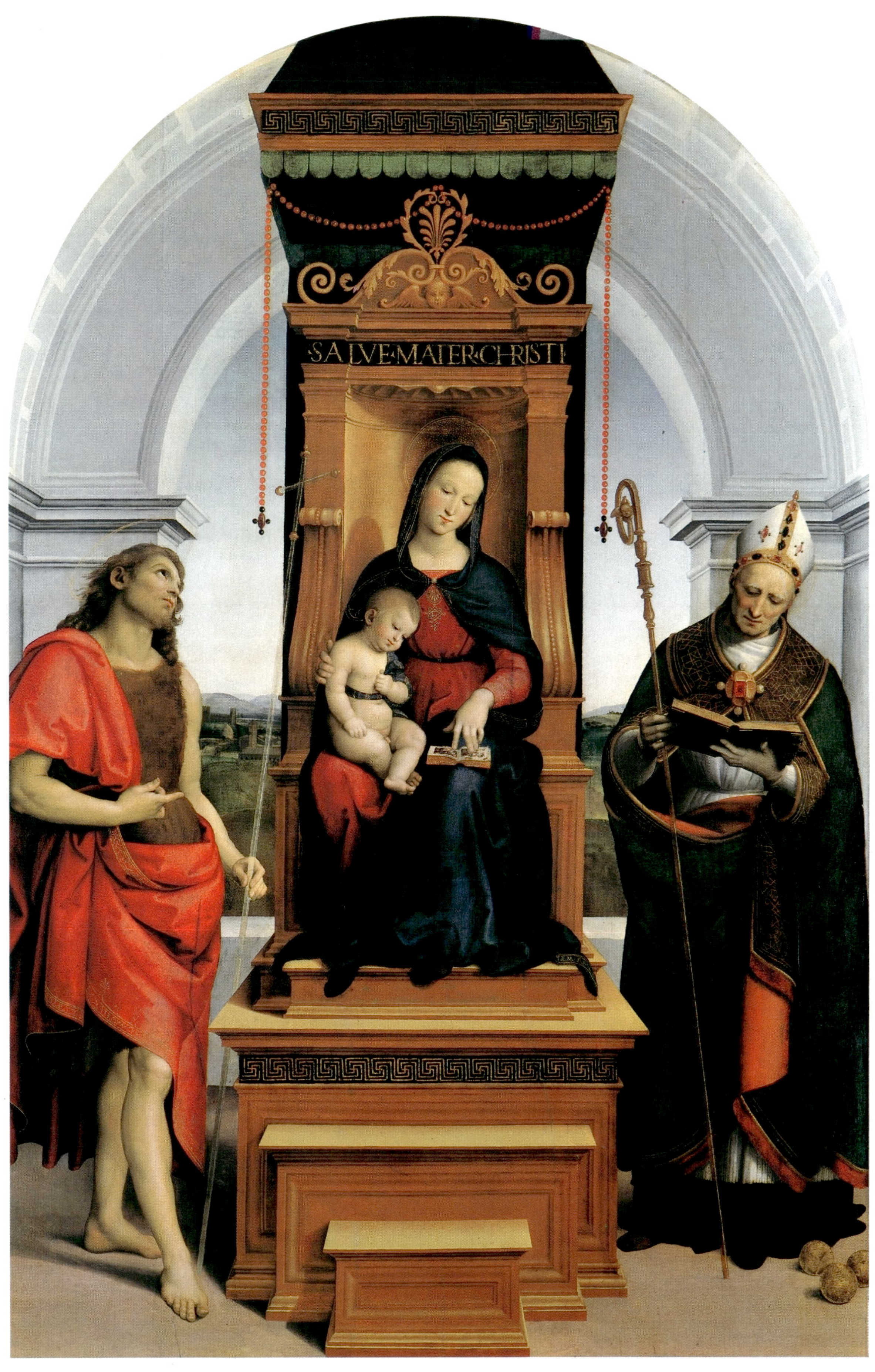

SALVE·MATER·CHRISTI

Raphael, 1483–1520

S. John the Baptist Preaching (predella panel)   (No. 6480)

Panel, 23 × 53 cm.
Purchased 1983

S. John the Baptist preaching originally formed the left part of the predella of the *Ansidei Madonna* (Plate 6), where it would have appeared immediately beneath the figure of the Baptist in the main altarpiece. It was accompanied by scenes showing the Marriage of the Virgin and a miracle of S. Nicholas of Bari, both of which disappeared in the mid-eighteenth century when the altarpiece was dismembered, perhaps because of their poor state of preservation.

Clearly the predella panel was carefully designed for the site it occupied on the altarpiece, and the light falls in both paintings from the same direction. The composition moves from left to right, towards the central scene originally shown on the predella, and on the far right in this painting S. John stands in isolation on a hillock. The painter was constrained to show his face partly in shadow, but in other ways he closely resembles the S. John of the main altarpiece. As though transported miraculously in time and place, he appears there bearing the same transparent cross, and again gesturing, not upwards but across the painting towards the Child who is the subject of his sermon. What differs most radically in the appearance of the saint is the treatment of the cloak, which swirls in convoluted folds in the predella, giving an almost Gothic sense of urgency to the figure, while also strengthening the asymmetrical composition at the right edge.

In comparison with the Baptist, his listeners form an earth-bound and weightier crowd, grave and attentive as they gather at his feet, or portrayed almost with an element of caricature at the far left. A group of four at the edge of the crowd, wearing contemporary dress and attending less conscientiously to the Baptist, would have strengthened the far-left edge of the predella. They are linked to the group around the Baptist by the subtle interpolation of the figure seen from behind who mediates between the two groups, observing with the spectator the whole action as it unfolds. Pink and green are the predominant colours of the draperies, relieved by a range of neutral tones, and each figure is carefully distinguished in dress and character, and portrayed with delicate strokes of the brush.

By the early sixteenth century the fashion for predellas was fast declining in Florence and the main artistic centres of Italy, but the impact of Florentine art is more apparent in the predella scene than in the altarpiece. Nowhere in the work of Perugino are there figures of such force and solidity as in Raphael's predella, nowhere a group organized with comparable ingenuity. Preaching and teaching were themes particularly well suited to the art of Raphael – untouched with violence, yet with their own inward intensity. From such subjects he was to create some of his most celebrated works, in the Vatican frescoes (fig. 1) and in the tapestry cartoons.

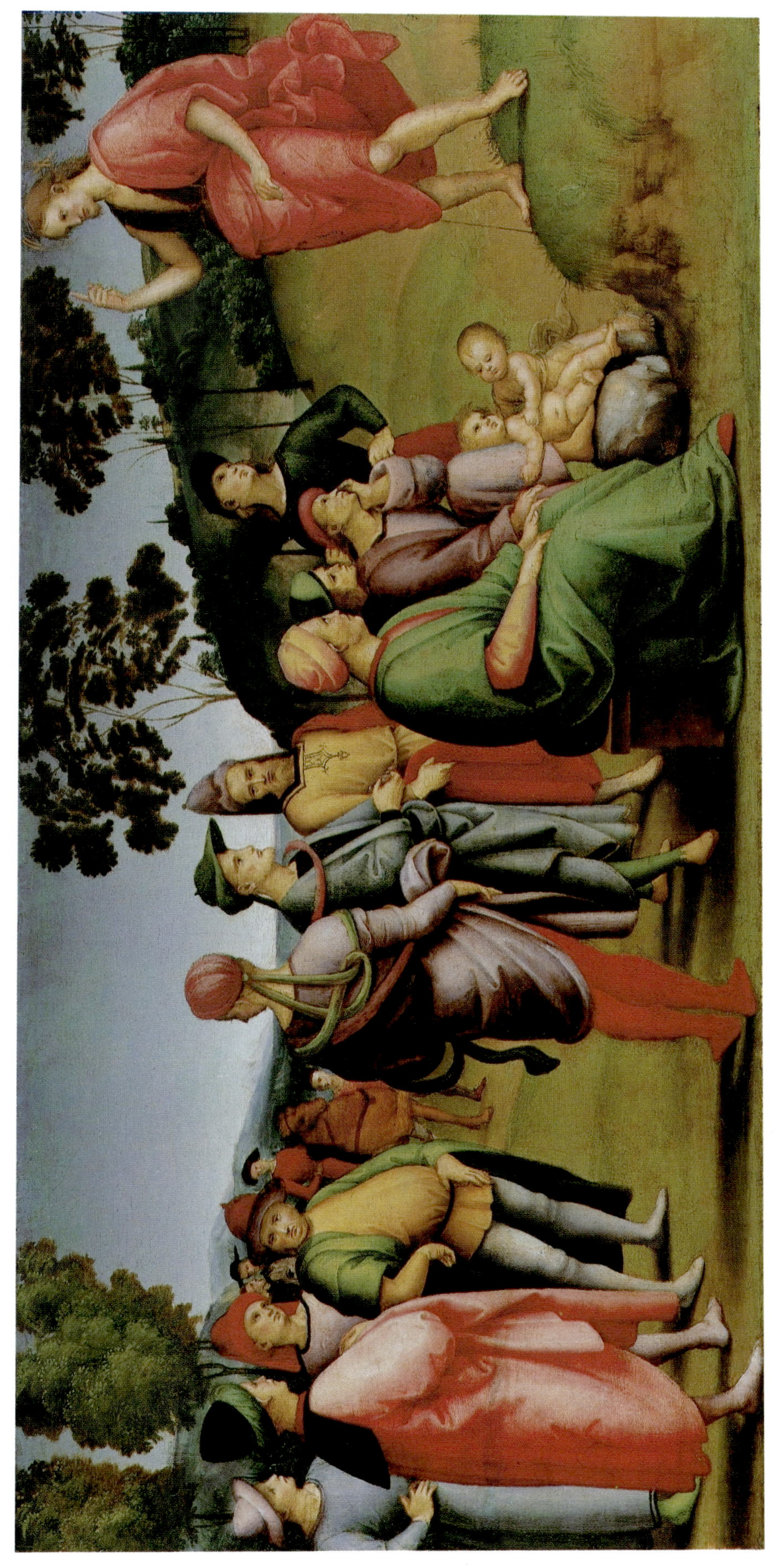

PLATE 8

Raphael, 1483–1520

S. Catherine of Alexandria (No. 168)

Panel, 71.5 × 55.7 cm.
Purchased from William Beckford 1839

The *S. Catherine of Alexandria* was painted probably about 1507, towards the close of Raphael's time in Florence, in the years which witnessed the creation of the first of so many famous masterpieces that were to establish the painter's reputation. This facility, the quality so notably foreign in the work of Leonardo and Michelangelo, was no doubt encouraged in Raphael by Perugino, and from his Umbrian background also derives that insistence on the outward expression of religious feeling, clearly apparent in the *S. Catherine*, which so deeply moved painters and critics from the seventeenth century onwards. The feeling was voiced by Raphael's first major biographer, Johann Passavant, in writing of the *S. Catherine* in the 1830s: 'To few has the power been thus given to represent an expression which partakes more of heaven than of earth.'

In handling the *S. Catherine* may seem over-meticulous and in colour even harsh, but this is perhaps the more apparent because in other ways the painting shows the deep transformation that had occurred in Raphael's work in the few years since the *Ansidei Madonna* (Plate 6) had been painted. Even its beautiful landscape, showing a gently flowing river, is more particular and more coherent than hitherto. The body of S. Catherine, supported on her heavy wheel of martyrdom, is now overwhelming in its three-dimensional presence and conceived at the same time in a pose of considerable complexity, a *contrapposto* of the kind in which Leonardo and Michelangelo delighted and which they alone were up till then able to carry out effectively. The body is turned towards the wheel while the head and legs of S. Catherine appear to recoil in a way that is expressive in this sacred context of the physical anguish of her martyrdom.

Knowledge of Leonardo lies behind this change in Raphael's conception of the figure, and a lost painting of *Leda*, copied by Raphael in a drawing, was of a single figure remarkable for the complexity of her pose. *S. Catherine* may also have been inspired by a variant of an antique statue, best recorded in the Medici Venus, and the increasing impact of classical art on Raphael's style is apparent here, not least in the treatment of the drapery. It was his response to antiquity, and to those particular statues that were the admiration of succeeding centuries, that was to ensure the enduring popularity of the painter.

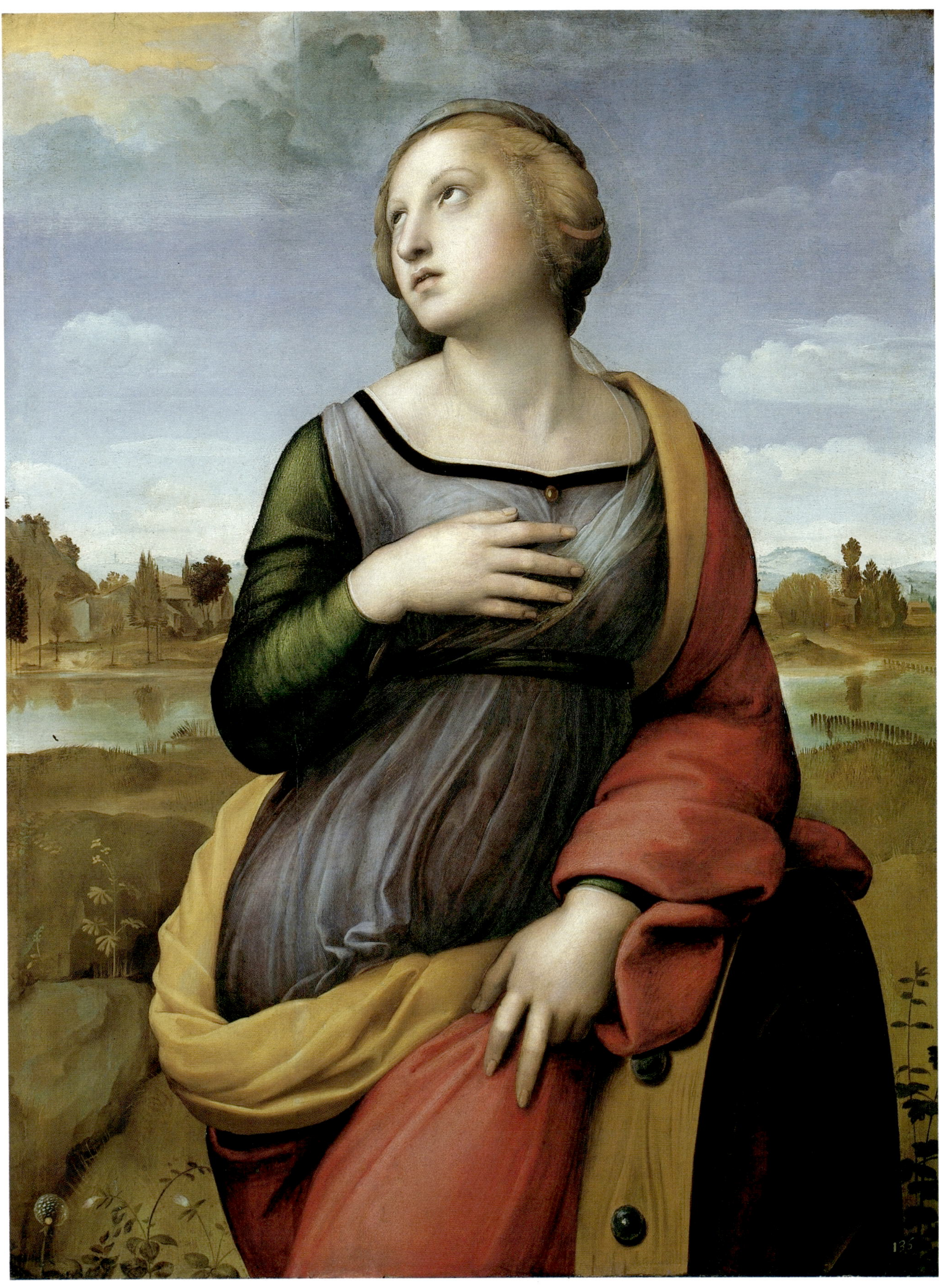

Raphael, 1483–1520

Pope Julius II   (No. 27)

Panel, 108 × 80.7 cm.
Purchased with the Angerstein Collection 1824

Julius II, the Pope who had called Raphael and Michelangelo to Rome for the decoration of the Vatican Palace, was nearing the end of a long and active life when Raphael captured this vivid likeness of him in a portrait which was probably carried out in the winter of 1511–12. Giuliano delle Rovere had been born almost seventy years earlier, in 1443, and he came into prominence in the Church when his uncle was elected Pope as Sixtus IV. He was made a cardinal in 1471 and headed a successful embassy to France. After the reign of his enemy, the Borgia Pope Alexander VI (1492–1503), he succeeded to the papacy on the death of the short-lived Pius III, and thereafter proceeded to enlarge the Papal States through military conquest and to transform the administration of the Vatican. It was Julius II who began the rebuilding of S. Peter's, of which Raphael and later still Michelangelo took charge after the death of Bramante in 1514.

Little of all this is outwardly manifested in Raphael's portrait of the Pope, which is surprising and moving as an image of introspection and melancholy. But, though the eyes may be downcast, the head bowed, and one hand grasping a handkerchief as though in mourning, the purposeful set of the mouth and the firm grasp of the left hand upon the chair leave no doubt as to the real character of the sitter. The winter of 1511–12 was not a time of contentment for the Pope, who had recently allowed his beard to grow as a sign of mourning after the capture of the city of Bologna.

The intimate character of the portrait is enhanced by the angle of the pose and of the chair – though, the viewpoint being relatively low, the dignity of the sitter is not compromised. Raphael seems to have taken the oblique presentation from the narrative fresco that he had painted in the Stanza della Segnatura in the Vatican where Julius is shown in the guise of Pope Gregory IX. In many later ecclesiastical and secular portraits the same pose was followed by other artists, and notably so in most of the great papal portraits of the next two hundred years. Successors of S. Peter, the popes accepted metaphorically the throne of the saint, and the chair on which Julius is seated is given particular prominence in Raphael's portrait. The polished finials of the back are shaped as acorns, alluding to the personal emblem of the Pope's family, the della Rovere ('oak' in Italian).

A new degree of subtlety and variety in Raphael's handling of oil paint (the freedom and softness in the rendering of the velvet cap, for example) emerged more clearly after the cleaning and restoration of the portrait in 1970, and likewise hidden touches of realism – the suggestion of grubbiness beneath the long fingernails and the hairs of fur protruding through the button holes in the cape. The painting was also substantially altered by the artist in the background where the curtain was originally decorated with a conspicuous pattern of large crossed keys, which are still clearly visible beneath the green layer that was intended to conceal them. Though the painting had been considered a copy, it became clear recently that this was indeed Raphael's original, the famous portrait that had been set up in 1513 in the church of S. Maria del Popolo in Rome to the applause of the painter's contemporaries.

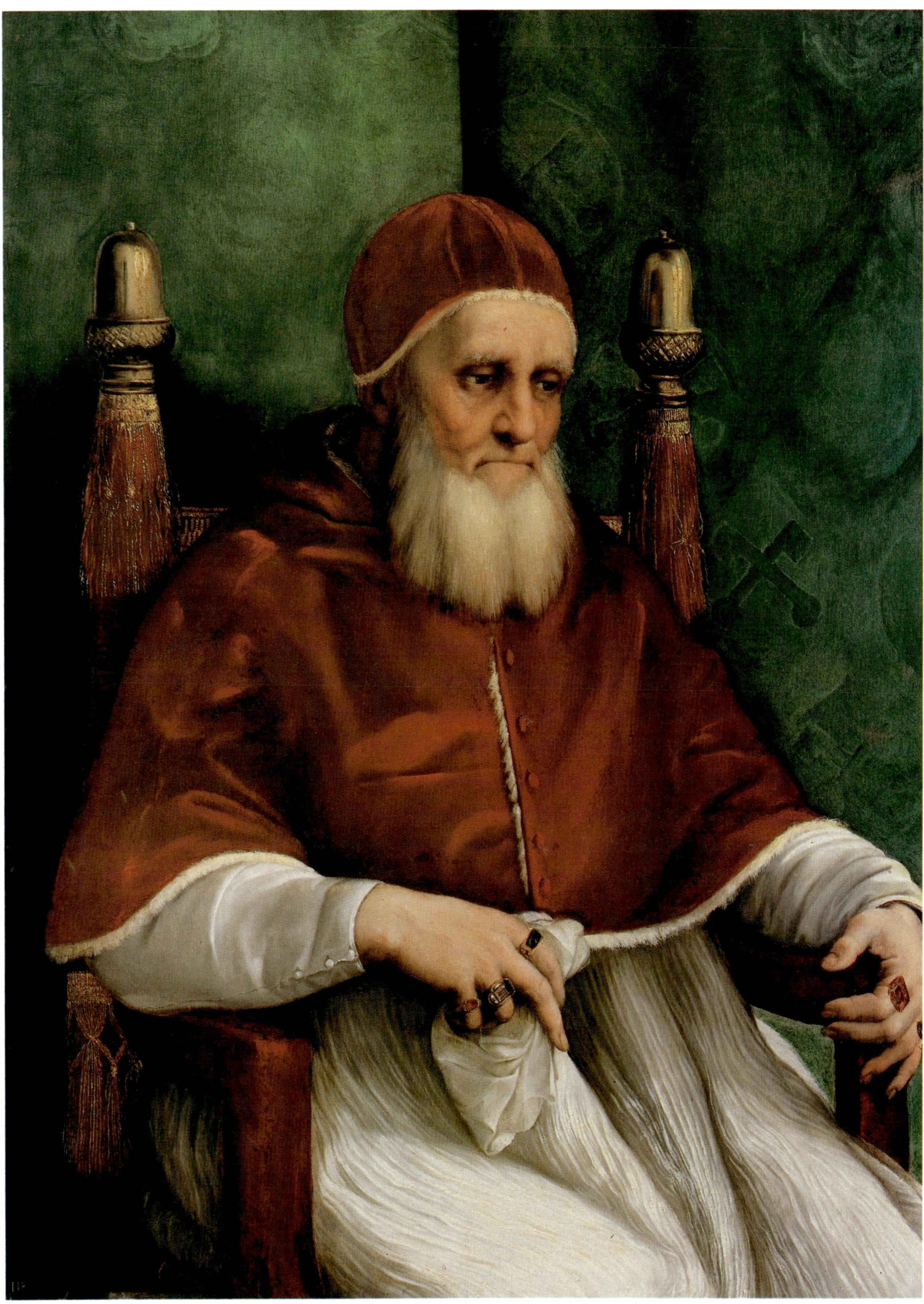

Giorgione, died 1510

The Adoration of the Magi (No. 1160)

Panel, 29.8 × 81.3 cm.
Purchased 1884

In the early years of the sixteenth century, painting in Venice underwent changes as considerable in their own way as those taking place in Florence, and the part played there by Leonardo fell in Venice to Giovanni Bellini in the very last years of his long life. The emphasis on texture and colour which becomes from this time onwards so pronounced a feature of painting in Venice conceals an intellectual distinction no less considerable than appears in the work of Michelangelo and Raphael, whose *Ansidei Madonna* (Plate 6) is exactly contemporary with Bellini's great altarpiece of 1505 in San Zaccaria in Venice. Vasari claimed that Giorgione knew of the work of Leonardo, who was briefly in Venice, and Bellini too must have been aware of the changes he had initiated, though many of the qualities which found a new fullness of expression in Bellini's late works had been inherent in his art from the beginning.

By the time that Bellini died in 1516, Giorgione, Titian and Sebastiano del Piombo had made their own contributions to the style of the new century. Giorgione is first mentioned in documents as active in 1507–8, when he painted a canvas for the Doge's Palace and frescoes on the exterior of the Fondaco dei Tedeschi; he is recorded as having died of the plague in 1510. Genius in his case was cut short by an early death, and Giorgione rapidly became a legendary artist, his works all the more coveted and intensified in poignancy.

The Adoration of the Magi is unusual amongst the paintings reasonably attributed to Giorgione in being a small-scale representation of a scene with many figures. It may even have been painted as a predella panel, as the asymmetry of the composition would also suggest, although predellas had become uncommon in Venice even by the later years of the fifteenth century. The painting shows many of the qualities apparent in Giorgione's larger paintings on canvas, though as a work in oil on panel the colouring is unusually saturated – isolated figures predominantly in blue on the left, balanced to the right by the richer and more varied colours of the kings and their attendants, who wear flamboyant costumes of the early sixteenth century. With the pageantry of the scene there also appears a certain timidity in the presentation. Seen from a relatively high viewpoint, the figures take on an appearance of vulnerability that is not found in, for example, Raphael's nearly contemporary predella panel (Plate 7), and the isolation of the holy figures contributes to the same impression.

Though the use of oil paint, in preference to tempera, was becoming widespread in Italy in the early sixteenth century, it had been a speciality of Netherlandish art, and the colder light in northern paintings sheds an even intensity on the colours and textures it serves to highlight. In Giorgione's work, oil became the means of recording the warm atmosphere in which his figures have their being. The textures and colours in *The Adoration of the Magi* – flesh and drapery and even the golden vessels being presented to the child – are broken and softened, thus imparting to the scene its sense of lyrical intensity.

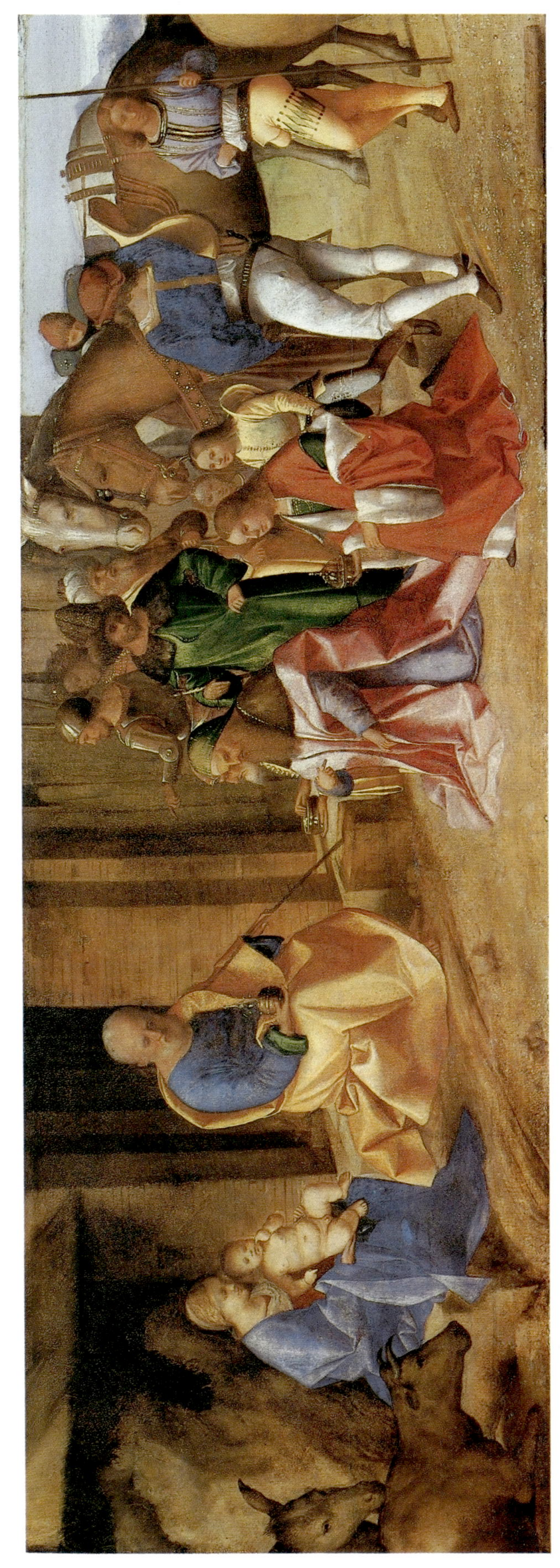

Giorgione, died 1510

Sunset Landscape with S. Roch, S. George and S. Anthony Abbot ('Il Tramonto') (No. 6307)

Canvas, 73.3 × 91.4 cm.
Purchased 1961

Giorgione's importance as a pioneer of landscape painting in Italy is manifest in the *Sunset Landscape*, which is generally agreed to be an early autograph work by the painter. The painting was discovered only in 1933, and it had belonged to the family of one of the sixteenth-century writers, Marcantonio Michiel, who had stimulated interest in the work of Giorgione. Though damaged and restored in parts, notably the white horse of S. George and the landscape below, much of the quality of the original is preserved.

The painting shows episodes from the lives of three saints, S. Roch in the foreground, S. George attacking the dragon to the right, and S. Anthony Abbot (a figure almost hidden in the rocks) on the far right. What is new in Giorgione's approach to such a subject is the subordination of the figures to the landscape, where they appear in naturalistic sequence as though seen by a traveller on his path around the shore of a lake. Roch was a saint of the early fourteenth century, who travelled extensively nursing the sick, and is shown here as a pilgrim, with his staff on the ground before him. He fell victim to the plague and is usually shown with a sore on his thigh. His remains were taken to Venice in 1485, when the Scuola of S. Rocco was founded. In Giorgione's painting S. Roch's leg is being tended by his companion, S. Gothardus. Their presence in the landscape is emphasized by a shaded bank upon which grows a young tree extending its branches into the sky above.

The combat of S. George, also a saint closely associated with Venice, is likewise reflected in the landscape, the curved precipice of rock that appears above the saint echoing the action of horse and rider as they bear down upon the dragon. S. Anthony, though scarcely visible, is accompanied by the devils in the shape of monstrous animals which haunted him in his desert retreat. They are small creatures in Giorgione's painting, and one has penetrated to the shore of the lake near S. Roch. S. Anthony was also a saint invoked as protection against the plague, and miraculous cures of the disease known as 'S. Anthony's fire' were attributed to him. It may be that the painting was commissioned at the time of the plague of 1504, which was succeeded not many years later by that to which the artist himself fell victim.

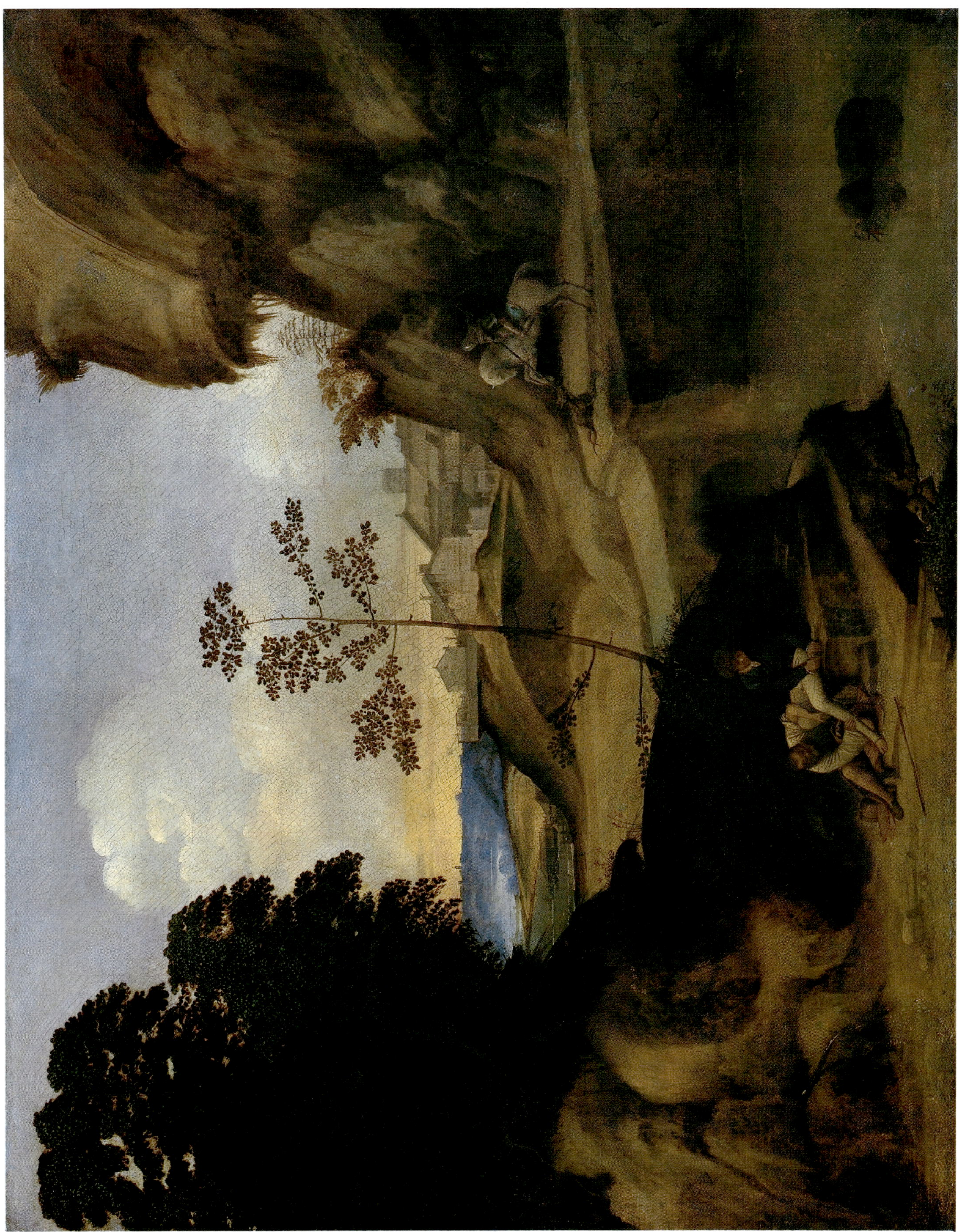

Titian, active before 1511; died 1576

'Noli me tangere' (No. 270)

Canvas, 108.6 × 90.8 cm.
Bequeathed by Samuel Rogers 1856

Little is known of the earliest years of Titian's life, and even the period of his birth is uncertain. He came from Pieve di Cadore in the Veneto, and according to his earliest biographers received his training in the studio of Giovanni Bellini. There followed a period when the young painter absorbed the influence of Giorgione, and the two artists worked together on the decoration of the exterior of the Fondaco dei Tedeschi in 1508.

The affinity in style between Giorgione and Titian was so great that a group of distinguished paintings has been attributed with almost equal justification to both artists. In 1511 Titian painted a series of frescoes in the Scuola del Santo in Padua, and the great masterpiece of his early years, the *Assumption of the Virgin* in the church of the Frari in Venice, dates from the years 1516–17. From then until 1576 his enormously productive career is better recorded, and the great majority of his paintings have survived – religious and mythological subjects, and portraits, commissioned by Venetians and by ruling families throughout Italy and Europe.

The *Noli me tangere* has been considered a painting started by Giorgione and completed by Titian, who gave the composition its final form. X-ray photographs show an earlier stage in the design in which the tree was smaller and inclined in the opposite direction, the buildings massed on the left, and Christ himself moving away from the Magdalen. Radical changes of this kind, however, are not infrequent in Titian's works, and the handling of the painting in its final form has that fluency and breadth which are characteristic of even the earliest works of the painter.

The preponderance of the landscape over the figures in a rendering of a sacred theme, though taken to a new extreme in Titian's painting, has its source in the latest works of Giovanni Bellini. In the *Noli me tangere* the encounter in the foreground is amplified on a larger scale in the landscape, where a tall tree supports the figure of Christ, a lower branch serving to enclose from a distance the upper part of his figure, and a nearby shrub stretches towards the tree, nearly touching the trunk.

Christ, having reappeared to the Magdalen to reassure her after the Resurrection, was at first taken by her to be a gardener. Here he has been recognized, and the Magdalen stretches forward eagerly to touch Christ. In a supremely eloquent pose (derived by Titian from an engraving of a female figure perhaps after Giorgione) Christ stoops compassionately towards her, at the same time withdrawing his cloak from her reach: 'Touch me not; I am not yet ascended to my Father' (John, 20: 17).

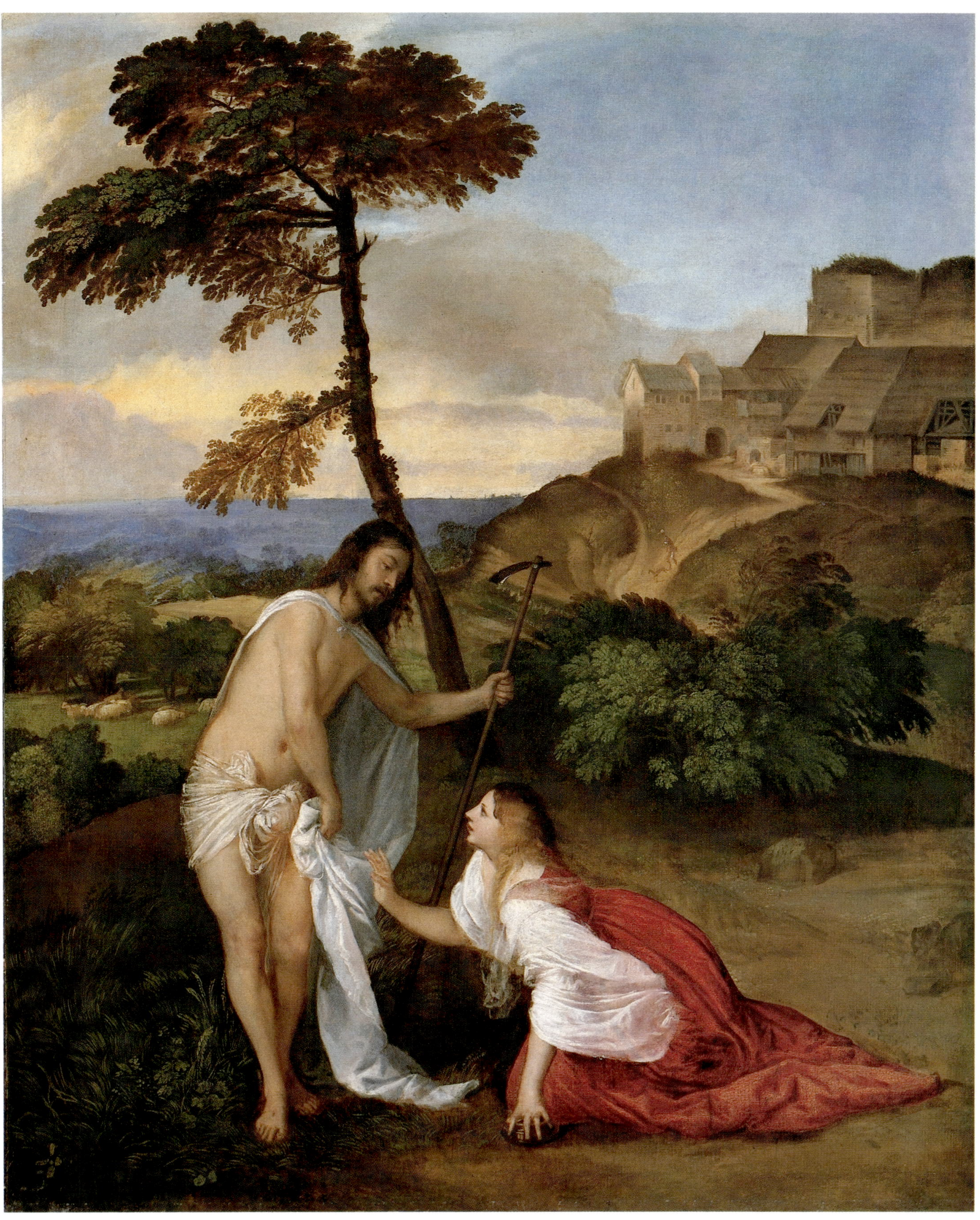

Titian, active before 1511; died 1576

The Holy Family and a Shepherd   (No. 4)

Canvas, 99.1 × 139.1 cm.
Holwell Carr Bequest 1831

Giovanni Bellini was celebrated as a painter of intimate, touchingly human representations of the Virgin and Child, several of which in the last phase of his career were ingeniously accommodated within a 'landscape' rather than the more conventional 'portrait' format. The landscape setting thus assumed greater importance than hitherto – its beauty and colouring enhancing the sacred figures in the foreground and dignified in turn by their presence. Titian developed these experimental paintings by Bellini in a long series of very influential works, of which *The Holy Family and a Shepherd*, probably of the early 1510s, would be the first. The attribution to Titian is not entirely beyond doubt, but weaknesses that have been discovered in the design of the figure of the Virgin may be merely accountable to the comparatively early date of the picture.

In all other respects, and not least in its bold and sonorous colouring, the painting is far from showing any timidity. The figures are grander in scale than in related works by Bellini, occupying most of the foreground space, though the canvas may have been trimmed. The subject is not an entirely traditional one, since two themes are ingeniously combined – a Holy Family in a landscape and a précis of the usually more elaborate Adoration of the Shepherds, with the ox and ass, present at the birth of Christ, included on the far left. The ass indeed is the first in the remarkable gallery of animal portraits created by Titian throughout the length of his active career.

In colour the brightest area is the blue and rose of the dress of the Virgin, the focus, with the Child, of the composition. The colours, however, have a pallid sheen with extensive white highlights defining the cascading folds of the dress and the smoother texture of the cloak. The white of the veil on which the child is displayed is matched on the right by the dress of the shepherd, who is separated from the Holy Family by the presence of a path in the foreground leading into the landscape. He and S. Joseph bear rough wooden staffs, giving the two figures a certain rustic, even Alpine, kinship, and underlining the role of S. Joseph as mediator between the shepherd and the Virgin.

S. Joseph's pivotal role is emphasized by the colours that he wears – a plain grey smock and a deep orange cloak – which form the richest note of colour in the painting. Stretching from his right shoulder to the left foot as it rests upon the path, the cloak bridges the centre of the composition and amplifies the mellow hues of the landscape in the background. Dawn has broken in the east, dispersing the night's grey haze, and an angel descends in the distance to tell the shepherds gathered on a hillside of the birth of Christ.

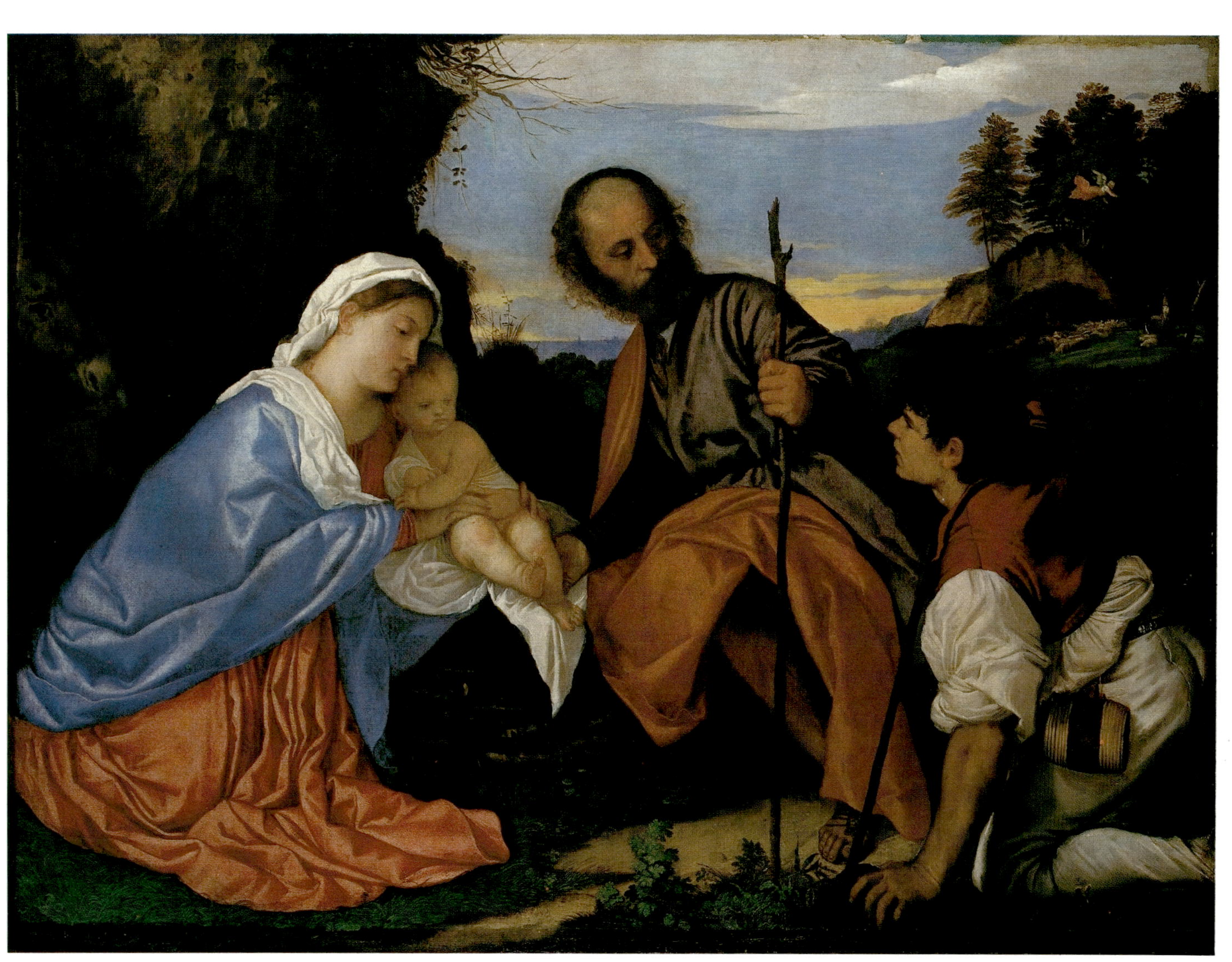

Titian, active before 1511; died 1576

Portrait of a Man   (No. 1944)

Inscribed: .T.V.
Canvas, 81.2 × 66.3 cm.
Purchased 1904

Portraiture played a central part in Titian's work at all stages of his career, and many new types of portrait were developed by the artist, whose extraordinary range of clients included a pope, an emperor, kings and noblemen, and fellow Venetians of all ranks. Titian's natural gifts as a portraitist are shown in this early painting, executed probably no later than the years 1510–15, which has become one of the most famous images of Renaissance man. Even in the seventeenth century, when it or a copy was in Amsterdam, the authority of the painting was well appreciated, and its influence can be traced in Rembrandt's *Self-portrait* of 1640, also in the National Gallery collection (No. 672, reproduced in this series as Plate 32 in Christopher Brown's *Dutch Paintings*).

The portrait follows a traditional pattern in the presence of a parapet, marking the division of the real and the painted world, but it is the painted image that seems to impose from beyond the parapet a surer sense of reality. The silky blue sleeve, softly dented as it unfolds over the ledge, is the most prominent feature of the painting, and by this daring reversal of the usual priorities of portraiture, the physical presence of the sitter seems all the more convincing. His wealth and elegance are revealed, as are the subtlety and virtuosity of the painter who has chosen to present him in such a manner.

The face is placed centrally on the canvas, the head and the eyes turned to face the spectator. The sleeve is thus stretched out to the right, but this asymmetrical arrangement has within it a sequence of checks and balances. The cloak extends the design to the left, while the vertical line of the cuff creates a hiatus on the right, before the emergence of the hand. The cloak projects above the cuff, echoing the contour of the chin. On the parapet appear the initials of the painter, the prominent letters T and V, placed not in the centre but as punctuation beneath the sleeve. They, too, play a prominent part in the design, seeming to suggest a personal relationship between the artist and the sitter, who is sometimes considered to be Titian himself.

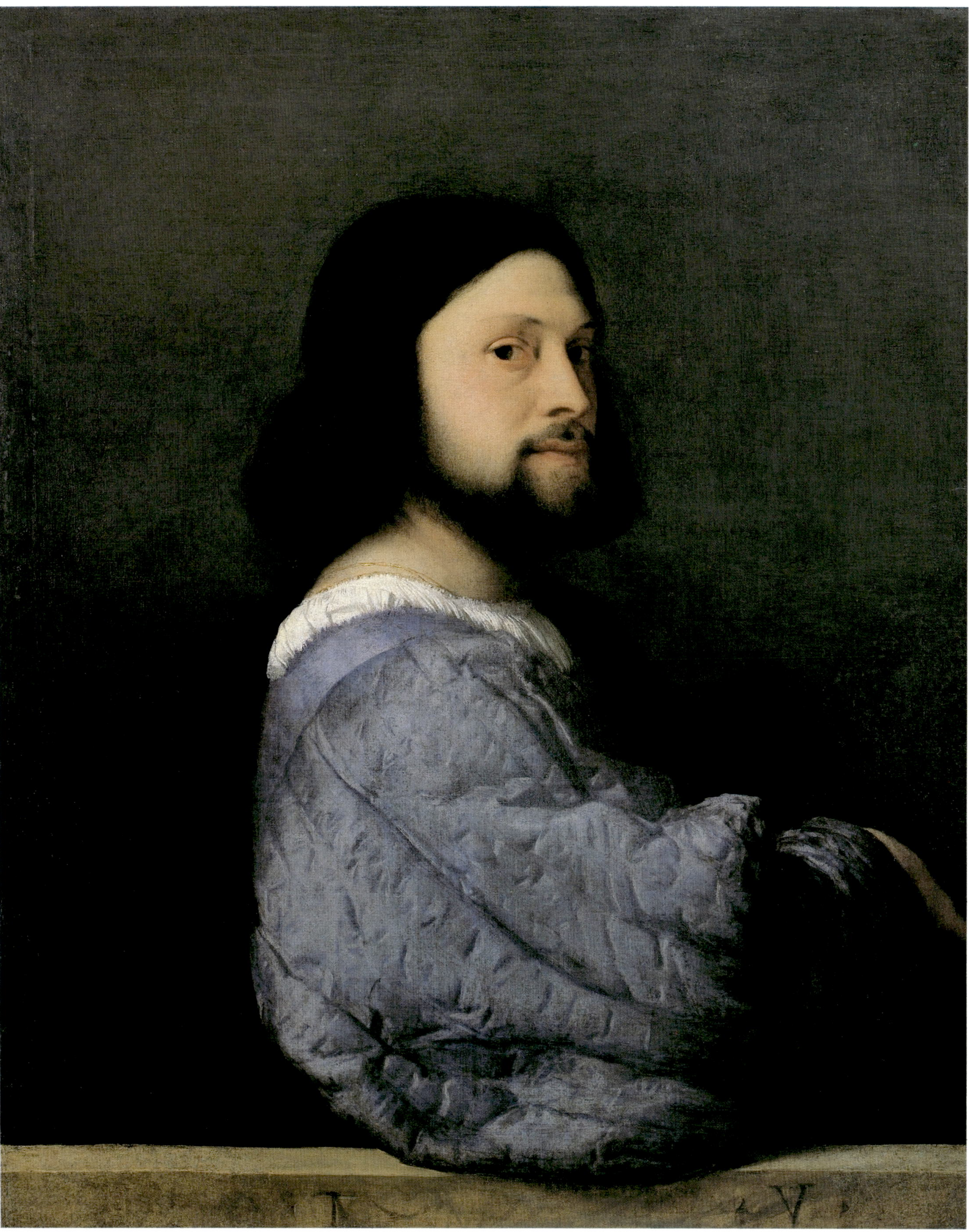

Titian, active before 1511; died 1576

Bacchus and Ariadne   (No. 35)

Signed: TICIANVS F.
Canvas, 175.2 × 190.5 cm.
Purchased 1826

An important feature of patronage in Italy in the early sixteenth century was a growing demand by ruling families for large-scale mythological paintings to decorate private rooms in their palaces. Not all the many artists approached for such paintings were eager to co-operate – or able to excel – in the depiction of subject-matter familiar largely from written sources, but for such commissions Titian created several of his greatest masterpieces.

Bacchus and Ariadne was ordered by Alfonso d'Este as one of a series of canvases for the decoration of a room in his castle at Ferrara, following the example of his sister, Isabella d'Este, who had created in Mantua a famous *camerino* to which Mantegna had contributed. Alfonso had admired in Rome the work of Michelangelo and had sought to engage Raphael and Fra Bartolommeo for paintings for his studio. Bellini produced one canvas for the series, *The Feast of the Gods* (now in Washington), Titian contributed three, the other two being *The Worship of Venus* and *The Andrians* (Prado, Madrid), and supplementary paintings were produced by Alfonso's court artist, Dosso Dossi (see Plate 37).

The series appears to have had no very obscure, or indeed moral, programme, but celebrated, rather, the pleasures of pagan life. The *Bacchus and Ariadne*, which Titian completed in Ferrara in 1523, is related to at least two classical sources – Catullus, and Ovid's *Ars Amatoria*, which describes Ariadne abandoned by Theseus on the island of Naxos, 'crying over the deaf waters', and the arrival of Bacchus with his followers: ' "Lo, here am I," said the god to her, "a more faithful lover. . . . For thy gift take the sky, as a star in the sky thou shalt be gazed at. . . ." He spoke, and lest she fear the tigers leapt down from the chariot.'

The splendid leaping figure of Bacchus, impelled with love for Ariadne, is the focus of Titian's composition. In the creation of such images of energy Michelangelo had set new levels of excellence, and here, as in other early works of Titian, a reference to the Florentine artist occurs in the outstretched left arm of the god (fig. 2). Ariadne in her loosened cloak of blue is more Raphaelesque and, as a figure seen from the back, her state of agitation is conveyed largely by her gestures. In the distance beyond the idyllic landscape the ship of Theseus appears sailing into the distance, while above the head of Ariadne a crown of stars is indicated in the summer sky. Contributing to her fear are the bizarre followers of the god, satyrs with a dismembered calf, a bacchante bearing cymbals, Silenus on his ass, and in the foreground a man coiled with snakes, recalling the famous *Laocoön* (fig. 3).

Almost more human than the distracted figures are the cheetahs, halted quietly before the chariot and shown as though commenting together on the scene. The barking dog is contrasted with them, and beside the dog a pile of yellow drapery has been introduced, showing the painter's widening mastery of colour, and a golden vase on its side upon the drapery. The colours of the painting were indeed the subject of a famous passage in the *Discourses* of Sir Joshua Reynolds, who noted the use of red for the scarf of Ariadne as the means whereby warmth was retained on the left of the canvas. He had remembered the detail from his study of the painting as a young man in Rome, little realizing that the painting itself would travel to England within a few years of his death.

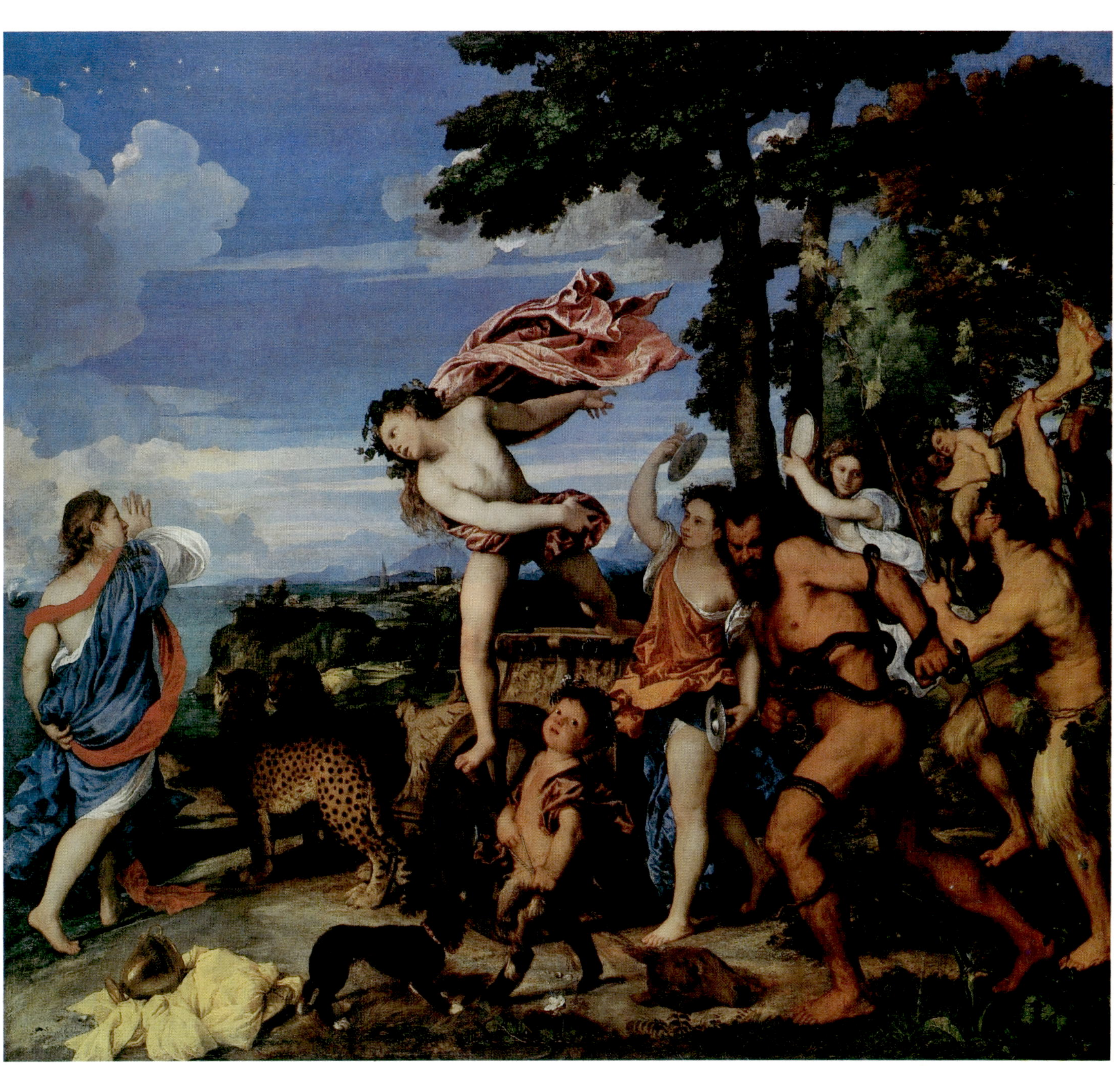

Vincenzo Catena, active 1506; died 1531

A Warrior adoring the Infant Christ and the Virgin (No. 234)

Canvas, 155.3 × 263.5 cm.
Purchased 1853

The new style of Giorgione and Titian was not immediately assimilated by every painter of distinction working in Venice in the early years of the sixteenth century, and even the latest works of Vincenzo Catena have a not unpleasing reticence that recalls an earlier age of Venetian painting. Catena was a close associate of Giorgione, and is recorded as a colleague in the inscription on the reverse of Giorgione's portrait of Laura of 1506 in Vienna. His contacts were amongst the humanists of early sixteenth-century Venice, and in one of his able portraits Catena has left the likeness of Giangiorgio Trissino, the first patron of Palladio.

His *Warrior adoring the Infant Christ and the Virgin* is probably of the same period as this portrait, dating from the later 1520s. The composition is that of a votive painting, the warrior portrayed in worship before the Virgin and Child, his belt and sword put aside under the guardianship of the dog. His semi-oriental appearance and the presence of the page with his horse recall the more conventional subject-matter of the Adoration of the Kings, and it has been proposed, not unreasonably, that the painting may well commemorate the conversion to Christianity of a knight of the eastern Venetian Empire.

The scene is represented with an engaging simplicity which had become rare since the age of Bellini and Giorgione. The figures are carefully separated from one another, each as carefully drawn and coloured, and the light, though mellow, falls with an even intensity throughout the painting. Bellini is the painter called to mind by figures of the Virgin and Child, and Carpaccio by the stage-like setting with its animals to each side. The partridges or quails on the left probably refer symbolically to the Church. The late date of the painting is betrayed only by the amplitude of the figures themselves, and the knight and his page in particular recall the work of Giorgione and the young Titian.

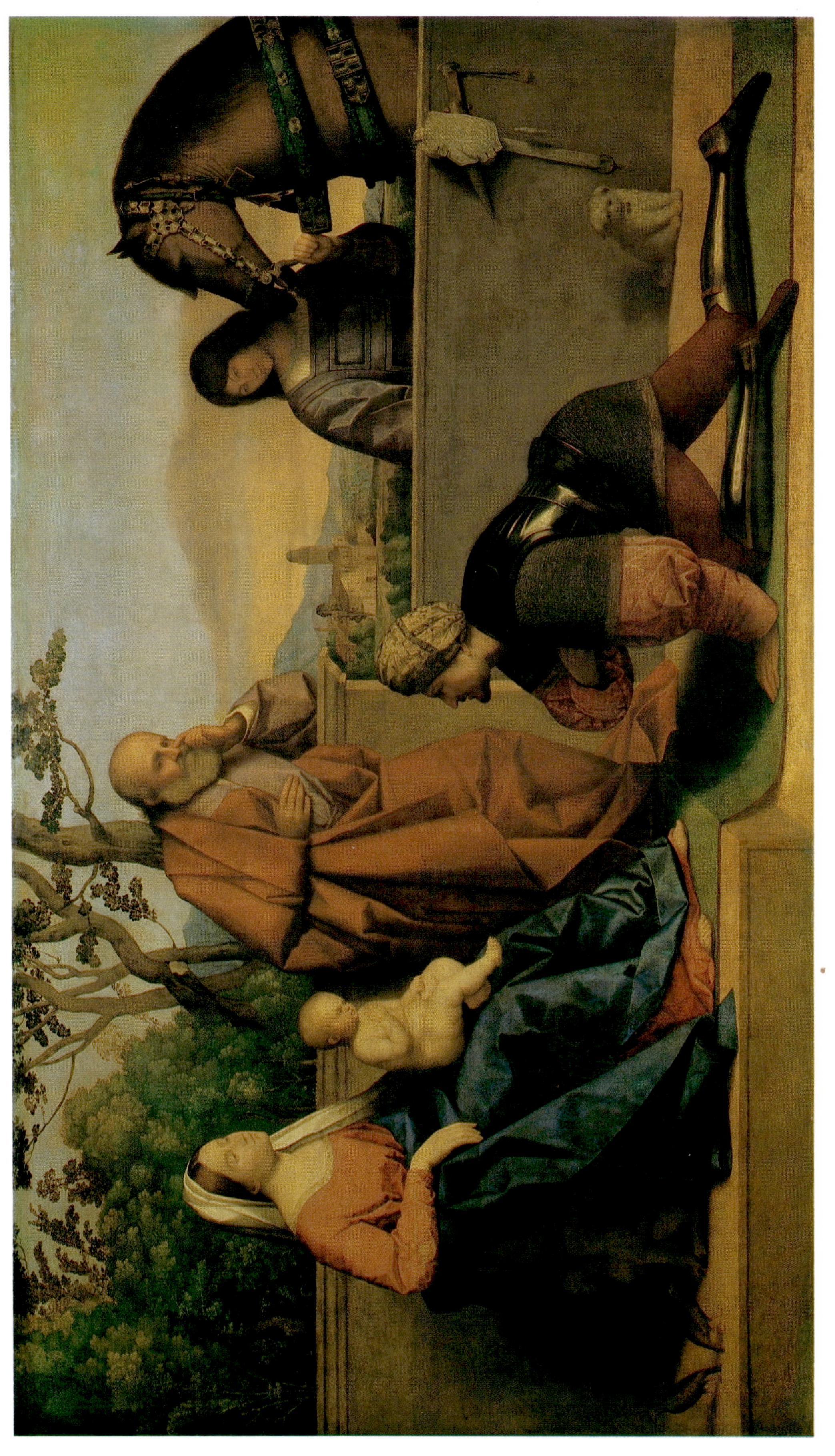

Palma Vecchio, active 1510; died 1528

Portrait of a Poet, probably Ariosto (No. 636)

Panel, 83.8 × 63.5 cm.
Purchased 1860

Palma Vecchio was active in Venice in the same years as Catena, but he was probably some years younger and he absorbed more readily the lesson of Titian's art. Certain of the later works of Catena (including Plate 16) have in the past been assigned to Palma in the earliest period of his activity. He was born Jacopo Negretti, near Bergamo, and had moved by 1510 to Venice where he adopted the name Palma and where he died. His work there included altarpieces, paintings of the Holy Family in a landscape of the type pioneered by Titian (Plate 13), and portraits, including representations of voluptuous blonde women, which became a speciality of Venetian painting in the early years of the sixteenth century.

The most famous and most accomplished of Palma's male portraits is the *Portrait of a Poet*, which understandably passed for many years as a work by Titian. Though by no means perfectly preserved, and discoloured by varnish, the painting clearly shows the influence of Titian in its handling and treatment of colour, while being smoother and blander in effect. The portrait was originally painted on wood, before being transferred to canvas in the nineteenth century and later restored to panel; Palma appears to have reconciled him-self only gradually to the use of canvas as a support.

The portrait probably dates from the mid-1510s, in which case it is a considerable amplification of a type of composition used by Titian in earlier portraits, and it may show the celebrated poet Ludovico Ariosto (1474–1533) at about the time of the publication of the first edition of his *Orlando Furioso* (1516). The son of the governor of the Castle of Reggio, he was at this time domiciled in Ferrara and a protégé of Cardinal Ippolito d'Este, the brother of Duke Alfonso.

In its rich costume the portrait recalls Titian's *Portrait of a Man* (Plate 14), though the effect is more fragmented and ornamental. The sitter wears a bracelet and a necklace of thin gold chains; a fur cape covers his coat of patterned rose-coloured silk striped with blue, and one hand is gloved. His left hand rests upon a book held upright, and behind the figure there appears a thicket of laurel (as in Giorgione's portrait of Laura), which must refer in this context to the real or desired fame of the sitter's writings. The mood of contemplation is established by the expression. The suggestion of a squint in the eyes is turned to advantage in the reflective glance away from the spectator, accompanied by a slight inclination of the head.

Sebastiano del Piombo, about 1485–1547

Madonna and Child with SS. Joseph and John the Baptist and a Donor (No. 1450)

Panel, 97.8 × 106.7 cm.
Purchased 1895

Sebastiano del Piombo was a Venetian by birth, and probably, like Titian, a pupil of Giovanni Bellini and Giorgione. His earliest works (including a *Salome* of 1510 in the National Gallery collection, No. 2493) are unmistakably Venetian in character, though less free in handling than Titian's first masterpieces. In 1511, however, Sebastiano moved to Rome, where he came under the spell of Michelangelo. Figures in his subsequent paintings are more sculptural in appearance and less warm in colouring, and some are based on designs supplied by Michelangelo for Sebastiano's guidance. He remained, however, famous as a portraitist, an art that had never seriously engaged Michelangelo. In 1531 he was made Keeper of the Papal Seal, whence the name *Piombo* derives.

The *Madonna and Child with SS. Joseph and John the Baptist and a Donor*, painted in Rome probably in the later 1510s, partakes of the intimate character of a portrait and shows the donor, who may represent Pierfrancesco Borgherini (see Plates 21 and 22), sheltering under the protecting arm of the Virgin. In its unusual shape the painting recalls the late Madonnas of Bellini, and remarkably rich colours are introduced to offset the traditional blue and rose of the Virgin's garments – a Michelangelesque green for her sash and a brilliant Venetian orange, bordered with yellow, for the lining of her cloak.

In pose and in colour the Virgin dominates the composition, resembling Michelangelo's deep-lapped sibyls on the Sistine ceiling, a heroic but also youthful Madonna controlling the Child and protecting the donor. The Child also recalls the Sistine ceiling, particularly the figure designed by Michelangelo to support the book held up for the prophet Daniel, but his function within Sebastiano's painting, perhaps greeting the donor, is not clearly defined. A note of domestic intimacy is introduced by the sleeping S. Joseph in the shadows to the right, while the near-monochrome figure of the Baptist on the left intercedes for the donor with the Virgin.

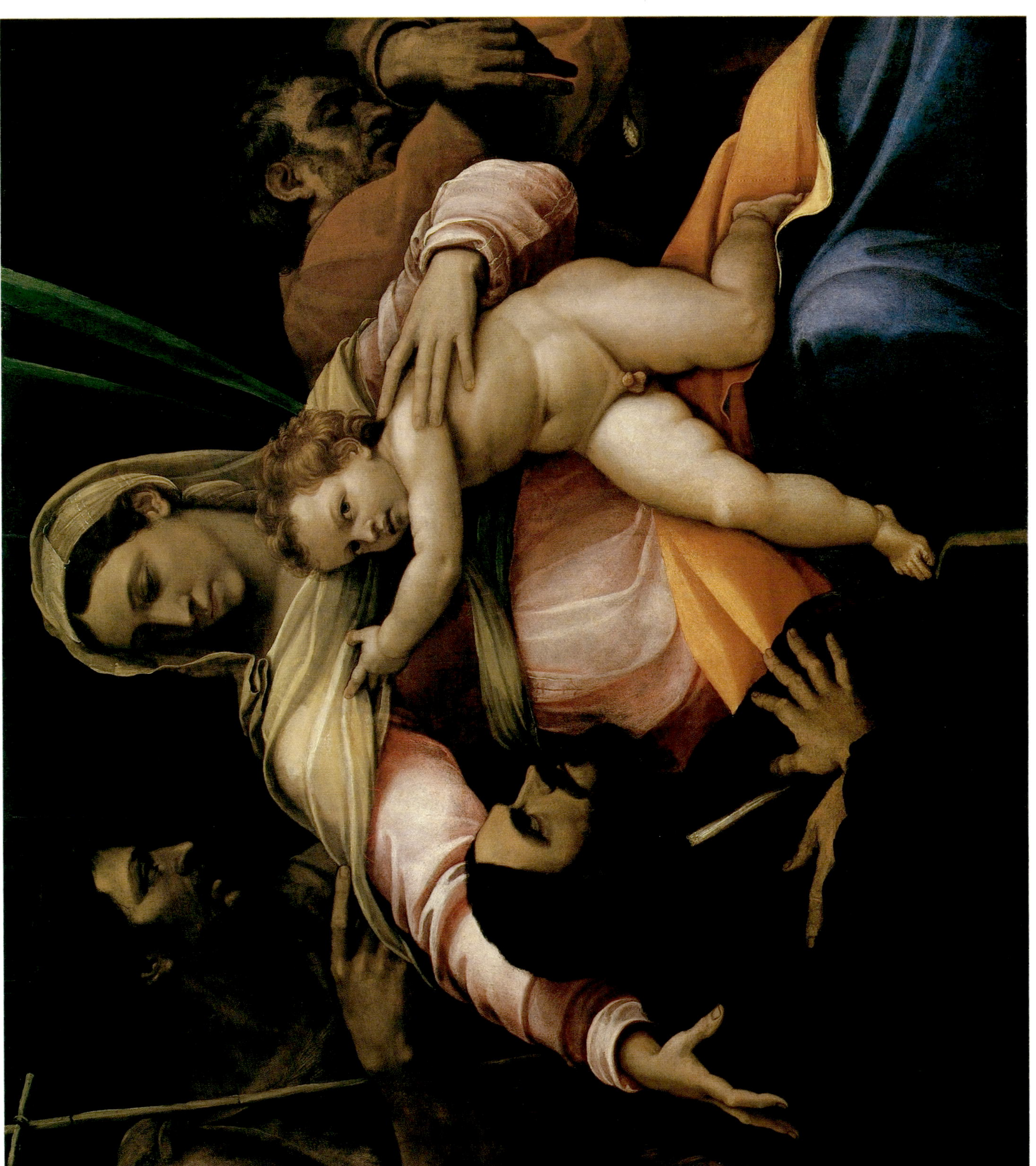

Sebastiano del Piombo, about 1485–1547

The Raising of Lazarus   (No. 1)

Signed: SEBASTIANVS . VENETVS. FACIE / BAT.
Panel, *c.* 381 × 290 cm.
Purchased with the Angerstein Collection 1824

Sebastiano's *The Raising of Lazarus* is one of the major landmarks of High Renaissance painting, a work on the most ambitious scale painted by the Venetian artist with the active collaboration of Michelangelo, who supplied drawings for the principal figures in the composition. The painting was commissioned by Cardinal Giulio de' Medici, a cousin of Pope Leo X, who had succeeded to S. Peter's throne on the death of Julius II. Giulio de' Medici, who himself became Pope as Clement VII in 1523, had been made Bishop of Narbonne in 1515 and it was as a gesture to his French see, which he was unlikely ever to visit though enjoying its revenues, that both Raphael and Sebastiano were approached for altarpieces. Raphael was at this time notoriously overworked by Leo X, though he eventually produced his latest masterpiece, *The Transfiguration* (Vatican Museum) for Cardinal de' Medici. This remained in Rome, however, while Sebastiano's painting was eventually sent to France. In the eighteenth century it was acquired by Philippe d'Orléans for the Palais Royal collection, and it thus came to England during the Revolution.

The miracle of the raising of Lazarus is described by S. John (11 : 33–44): 'Jesus . . . again groaning in himself cometh to the grave. . . . Martha, the sister of him that was dead, saith unto him, Lord, by this time he stinketh: for he hath been dead four days . . . he cried with a loud voice, Lazarus, come forth. And he that was dead came forth, bound hand and foot with graveclothes. . . .'

Poised on a dais of stone jutting into the painting, the superhuman figure of Christ dominates the scene, recalling Lazarus to life as God the Father had been shown by Michelangelo creating Adam on the Sistine ceiling. As they turn away from the bizarre and powerful body of Lazarus, so the by-standers address themselves in wonder to Christ, Martha in the centre and on the left the apostles, with S. Peter in the foreground in an exaggerated pose that calls attention to his veneration. Through the figure of S. Peter the papacy, about to witness the dawning of the Reformation in northern Europe, is associated with this dramatic manifestation of miraculous resurrection.

The blue and rose of Christ's garments isolate him from the surrounding figures, though a grey-blue is used for the robe of S. Peter. The colours have a Venetian intensity, but prominent white highlights add a suggestion of sculptural firmness to draperies and the limbs beneath. The shades of green and grey, yellow and muted orange that punctuate the encircling crowd are those familiar from the frescoes of Michelangelo. Narrative, however, was not where Sebastiano's real strength lay, where in fact he welcomed guidance, and a more complex subject, like the Transfiguration, would clearly have defeated his powers. It is rather as a collection of individual figures that *The Raising of Lazarus* succeeds, with the accompaniment of its haunting landscape, like an extra presence in the background, where the ruins of antiquity appear and a group of washerwomen laundering at the river bank.

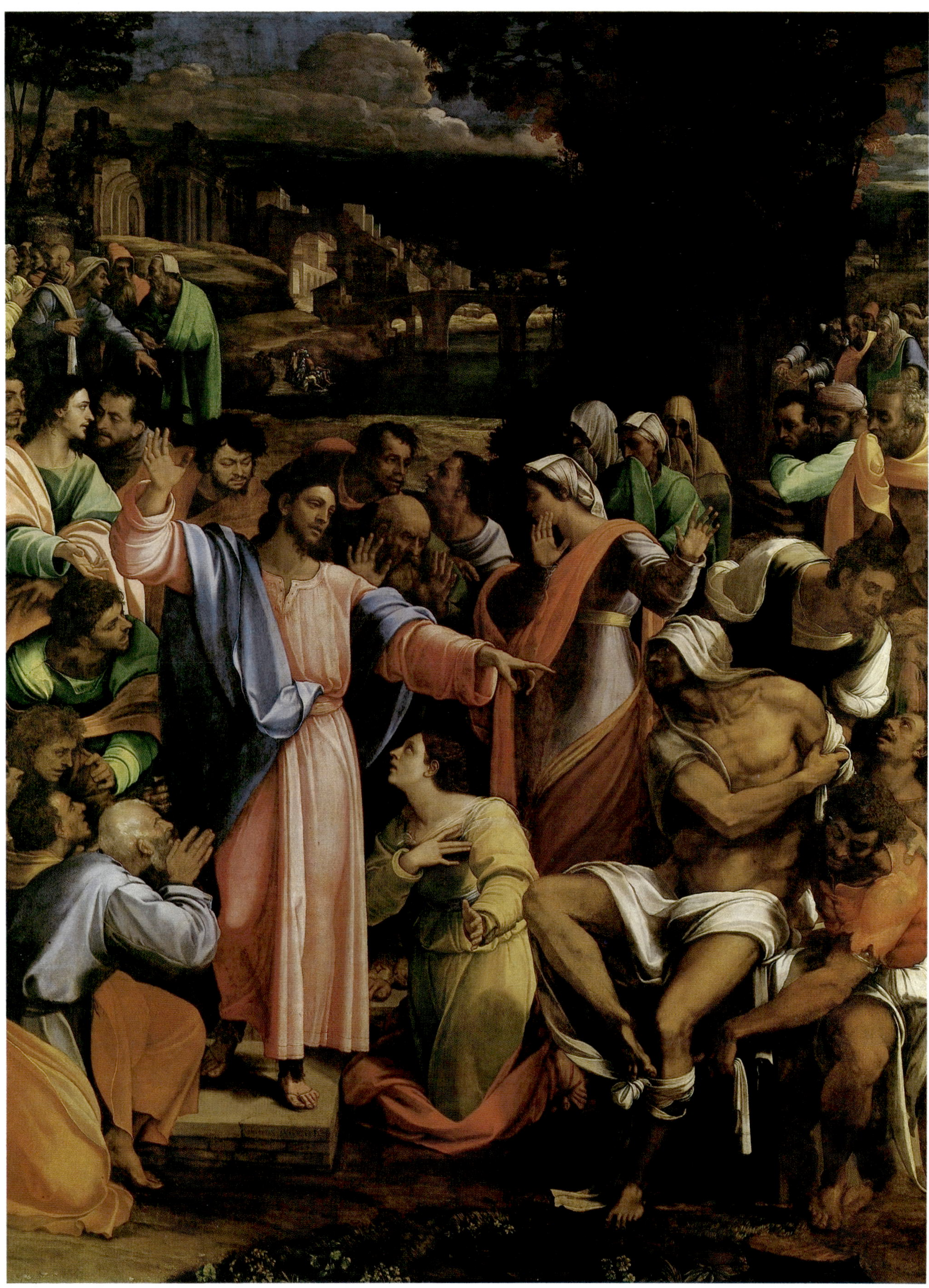

Andrea del Sarto, 1486–1530

Portrait of a Young Man (No. 690)

Signed with the artist's monogram
Canvas, 72.4 × 57.2 cm.
Purchased 1862

Though painting in Florence was directly impoverished by the return of Leonardo to Milan in 1506, and the departure not long after of Raphael and Michelangelo for Rome, the genius of the native school, represented by Fra Bartolommeo, Andrea del Sarto, Pontormo and Bronzino continued to flourish until the mid-century. Andrea del Sarto was born in Florence in 1486, the son of a tailor, as his name implies, and except for a visit to France in 1518–19, following Leonardo at the court of Francis I, he remained in or near his native town until his death, painting mainly religious works and a handful of portraits of more uneven quality. A painter extravagantly admired in the eighteenth and nineteenth centuries, Sarto was, above all, appreciated for his subtle and subdued colour harmonies, the soft and coherent tonality of his paintings – his most obvious debt to Leonardo – and the peculiar vivacity of his figures, based for the most part on his many justly famous life drawings in chalk.

The *Portrait of a Young Man*, probably of around 1517, is perhaps his best-known work in portraiture, a daring experiment with an informal pose that is at the same time carefully controlled in design. The arm of a chair here serves in place of the more usual parapet to distance the sitter from the spectator and to stabilize the composition. The back of the chair rises in the shape of a pyramid with a rectangular projection at the summit, lifting the composition at the base and echoing the pose of the figure. Sarto experimented with more conventional designs for the portrait in a series of preliminary drawings, and these make it clear that the sitter holds in his hands a book, an area in the painting that is damaged and not fully intelligible. Dressed informally but wearing a hat, the sitter has been interrupted in study, and he turns guardedly to face the spectator.

As in Titian's early *Portrait of a Man* (Plate 14), the head, underscored by the white of the shirt which rises at the left shoulder as the sitter turns, is juxtaposed with a wide billowing sleeve, but in this case the material is neutral in tone, lively in handling though in texture unexciting, and it is the head, even the mind itself, which dominates the portrait. Strong dark shadows, like those employed by Leonardo, impart to the face its intensity of expression, but the features themselves are by no means softened as Leonardo might have desired. The shadows emphasize the angularity of the features in a way that is expressive of the intellect and character of the sitter.

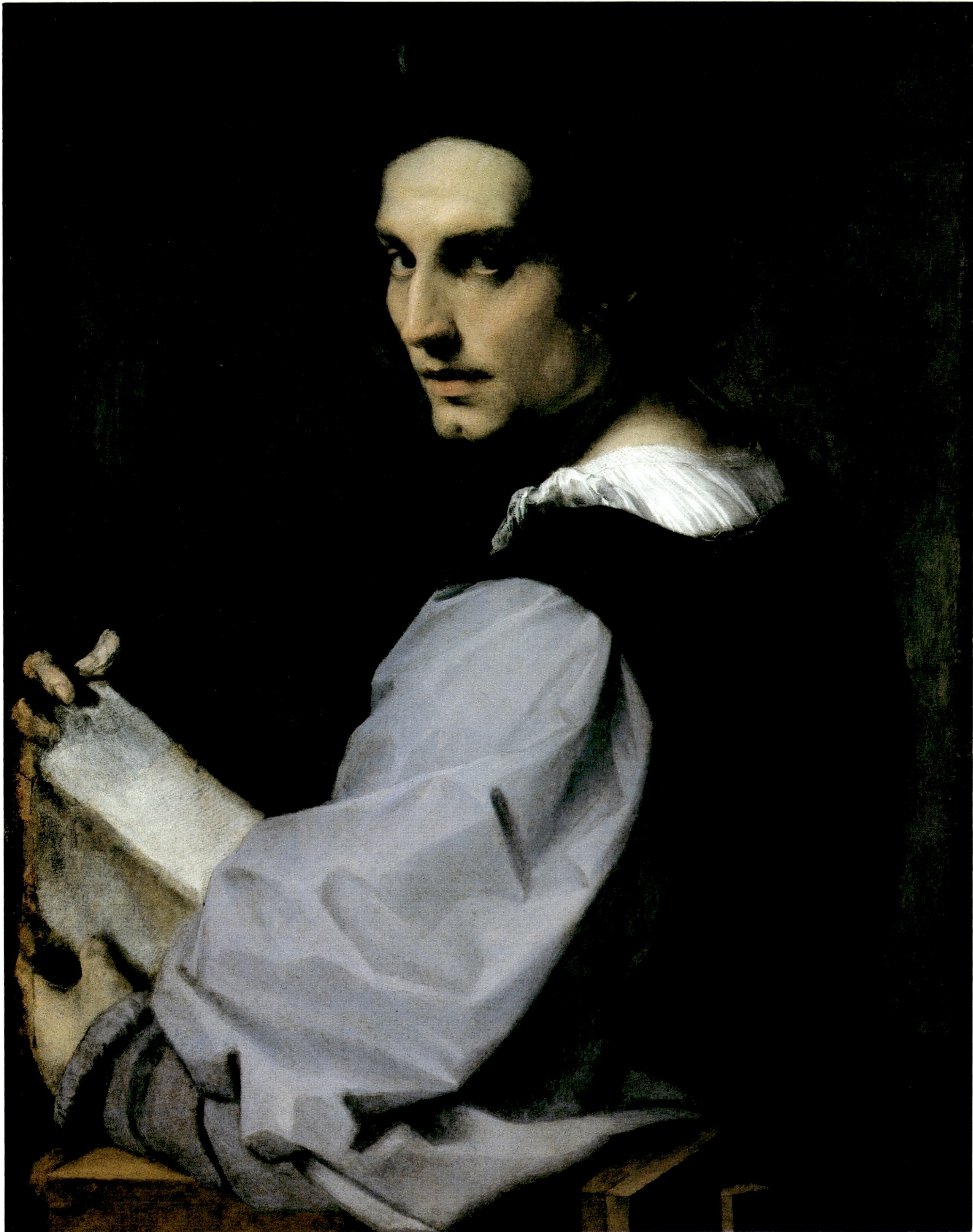

Pontormo, 1494–1557

Joseph sold to Potiphar (No. 6451)

Panel, 61 × 51.6 cm.
Purchased 1979

Jacopo Carucci, from Pontormo in Tuscany, was a younger contemporary and probably also a pupil of Andrea del Sarto, and many of the characteristics of Sarto's style were exaggerated to an irrational extreme in the work of the younger man. A propensity to melancholy and paranoia was indeed basic to Pontormo's personality, and the exaggerated expressiveness of his work, which has contributed to its present-day popularity, represents a partial negation of the values of Leonardo and Raphael. The energetic art of Michelangelo, on the other hand, was more deeply appealing to the reclusive artist, and its influence is combined in his work with that of German art, equally expressive of physical energy and known to Pontormo through the medium of engravings.

The *Joseph sold to Potiphar*, together with the *Joseph with Jacob in Egypt* (Plate 22) formed part of a series of bedroom decorations in the Palazzo Borgherini in Florence illustrating the story of Joseph, on which Pontormo collaborated with Sarto and two less famous Florentine painters, Francesco Granacci and Bacchiacca. The majority of the paintings appear to have decorated the bed itself, two chests and the panelling above, and they were commissioned to celebrate the marriage of Pierfrancesco Borgherini, who is perhaps shown in Sebastiano's painting (Plate 18), and Margareta Accaiuoli, which took place in 1515. Borgherini was a banker and merchant, established in Rome and Florence, and the subject of Joseph and of his successful, if bizarre, career in Egypt was not without relevance to the patron. Joseph's life had also mirrored that of Christ, as was underlined in the paintings, and this provided a moral context for the decoration, which also touched upon the subjects of chastity and the interpretation of dreams.

Such a programme was evidently sympathetic to Pontormo's lively imagination with its brilliant perception of colour, design and handling, through which one of the most famous works of early sixteenth-century Florentine art thus came into being. Dressed in yellow and hat in hand, the young Joseph stands before the grand figure of Potiphar, who is encircled by his dependants. On the left the scene is one of commotion as the Ishmaelites receive payment for selling Joseph into slavery in Egypt. One stoops to retrieve a fallen coin as money is passed around in a hat. The New Testament parallel for the subject was the Betrayal of Christ. In the background is the fantasy palace of Potiphar with asses entering the vestibule and spectators gathering before its curved and circular windows. A statue of Charity on a pedestal immediately above the figure of Potiphar underlines the message of the scene.

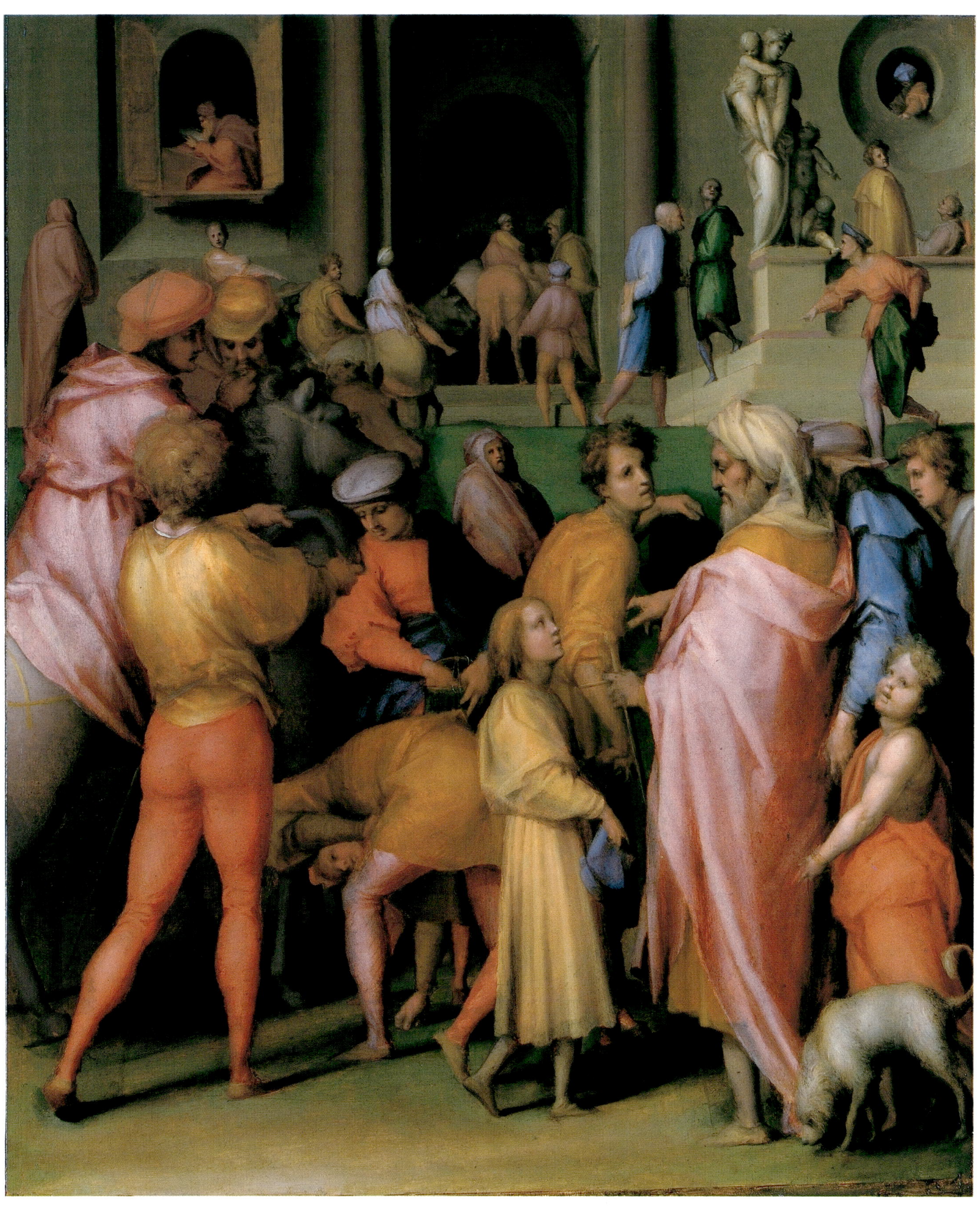

Pontormo, 1494–1557

Joseph with Jacob in Egypt (No. 1131)

Panel, 96.5 × 109.5 cm.
Purchased 1882

Joseph with Jacob in Egypt, from the same scheme of decoration as *Joseph sold to Potiphar* (Plate 21), shows the conclusion of the story of Joseph. The most ambitious of the panels provided by Pontormo, it may have been painted somewhat later than the others, and commissioned in acknowledgement of the success of Pontormo's earlier contributions. It was praised by Vasari as a 'painting rightly regarded by all craftsmen as the most beautiful picture that Pontormo ever executed'.

Several episodes of the story are shown in the painting, and Joseph himself, dressed in brown and mauve, appears four times: introducing his father, Jacob, to Pharaoh in the left foreground; seated on a wooden chariot and receiving a message or petition (bottom right); mounting the staircase in the right background with one of his sons; and presenting his sons to the dying Jacob (upper right). In this last episode of the story Jacob crossed his arms and blessed the younger son Ephraim with his right hand, and this was commonly taken to symbolize the eventual success of the Gentiles at the expense of the Jews. The introduction of Jacob to Pharaoh had already been shown by Granacci in the immediately preceding panel in the series, and it was perhaps for reasons related to the subsequent history of the Borgherini family that Pontormo was asked to repeat this incident and to continue the story in one scene up to the moment of Jacob's death.

The resulting painting shows a considerable development of the fantasy of Pontormo's earlier panels, with the same blending of tenderness and turbulence in the treatment of the figures. The improvised architecture gives a sense of exotic unreality to the scene, though the buildings in the landscape, far from being Egyptian, are closely derived from an engraving by Lucas van Leyden. They are accompanied by life-like statues in implausible positions which punctuate the action of the painting. A live boy dances on the column decorating the chariot of Joseph, and three others are reined before it. It may be the announcement of Jacob's imminent arrival, or of his final illness, that agitates the seated figure of Joseph, causing such disturbance in this corner of the painting. He turns to the kneeling figure beside the chariot, disregarding the colourful crowd in the middle distance and the spectators in the landscape beyond.

Strangest of all in the painting is the small figure of a boy in contemporary dress seated on the steps before the chariot and exchanging words with one of Joseph's pages. As Vasari recorded, this is a portrait of Pontormo's protégé and favourite pupil, the young Bronzino (see Plate 23), who is thus given a part of his own in the story Vasari recorded no surprise that he should have been portrayed in the painting but, becoming more specific in his praise, described the skill of Pontormo 'in the vivacity of the heads, in the organization of the figures, in the variety of the poses, and in the beauty of the invention'.

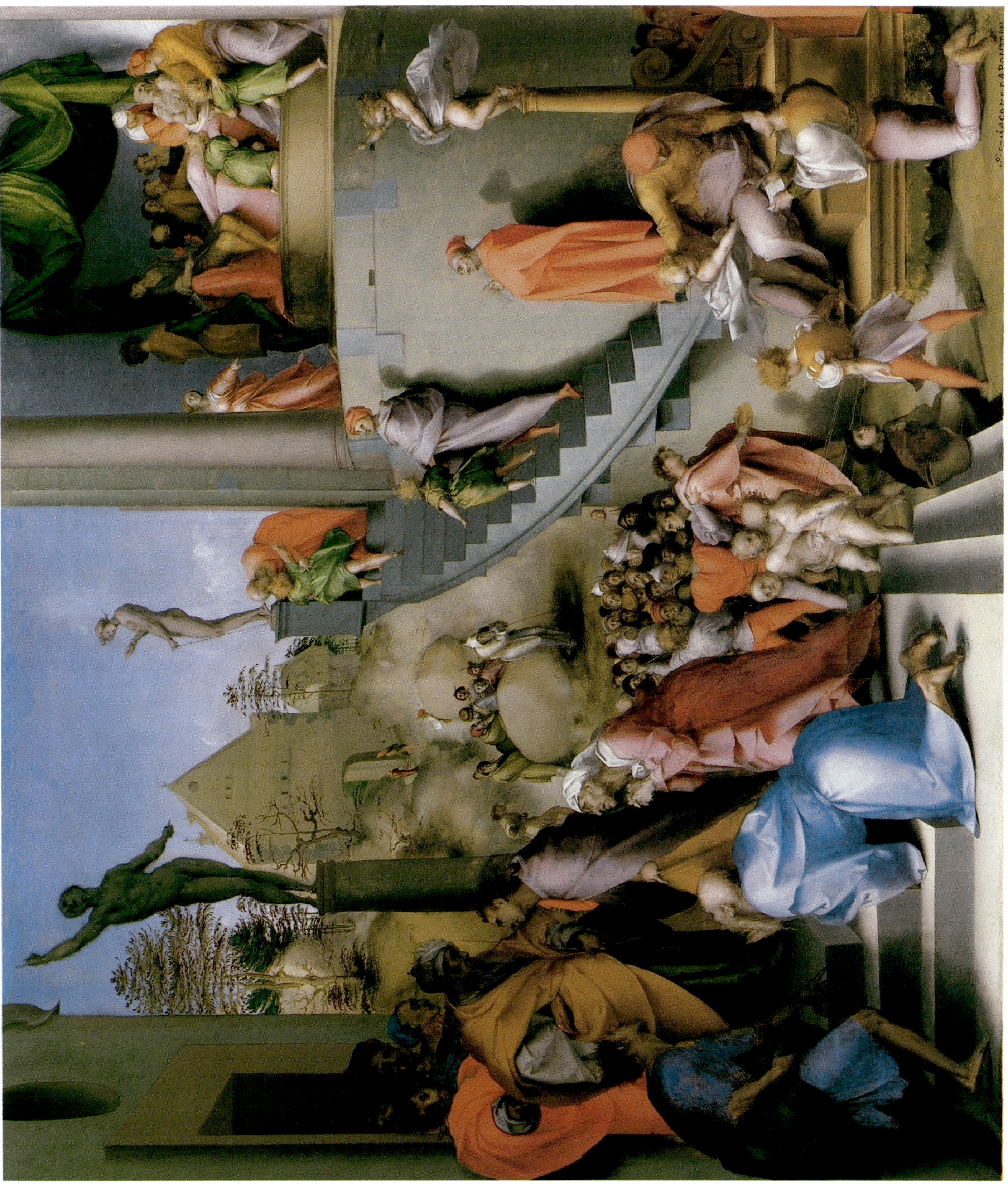

Bronzino, 1503–1572

An Allegory of Venus and Cupid (No. 651)

Panel, 146 × 116 cm.
Purchased 1860

Pontormo's favourite pupil and protégé, Agnolo di Cosimo, called Bronzino, who is pictured as a boy in Pontormo's *Joseph with Jacob in Egypt* (Plate 22), became an equally talented painter, the leader of a younger generation whose aims Pontormo himself found increasing difficulty in realizing. Designs that grew ever more complex, figures in poses of unexampled complexity, and paint itself taking on the character of marble in fulfilment of the example of Michelangelo created few apparent difficulties for Bronzino, who excelled in addition in portraiture, creating the series of immaculate images of Cosimo I, the first Grand Duke of Tuscany (1537–74), his family and court, for which the painter has always remained justly famous.

The painting known as *An Allegory of Venus and Cupid* – a title concealing doubt about its true meaning – is one of Bronzino's very few surviving mythologies and a masterpiece revealing the full complexity of his style. It is probably the painting described by Vasari as having been sent as a present to King Francis I of France, who died in 1547, 'a picture of singular beauty . . . in which was a nude Venus with Cupid who was kissing her, and Pleasure on one side with Folly and other Loves, and on the other side Fraud, Jealousy, and other passions of Love'.

Venus, Cupid, and Folly, the boy to the right holding roses and wearing an anklet of bells, are the three main actors in the scene, each shown in a pose of considerable contortion. Venus recalls in the disposition of her legs and right arm the Madonna of Michelangelo's early painting, the Doni tondo (Uffizi, Florence), the legs in both paintings marking the base line of the composition, but the pose is otherwise ingeniously adapted by Bronzino to convey the impression of erotic abandonment. Venus bears in her left hand the attribute of a golden apple, the gift that Paris had awarded for her beauty, and with her right hand she disarms Cupid, holding aloft as he kisses her an arrow taken from his quiver.

The polished surface of the painting conceals here a significant change which is revealed by X-ray photographs. Originally Venus was shown caressing the hair of Cupid, whose own body seems to have been less prominently displayed. So strikingly are the lovers presented and executed that the moral commentary upon their transitory rapture, as in Veronese's *Allegories of Love* (Plates 47 and 48), seems of secondary importance. Pleasure on the right, hiding behind Folly, carries a honeycomb in one hand and in the other her own reptilian tail equipped with a sting; the screaming figure of Jealousy on the left tears her hair, and Time at the top of the composition stretches across the panel to tear away the drapery held up by a figure probably representing Fraud, a mask-like face directing the action of the hands but lacking a back to its head.

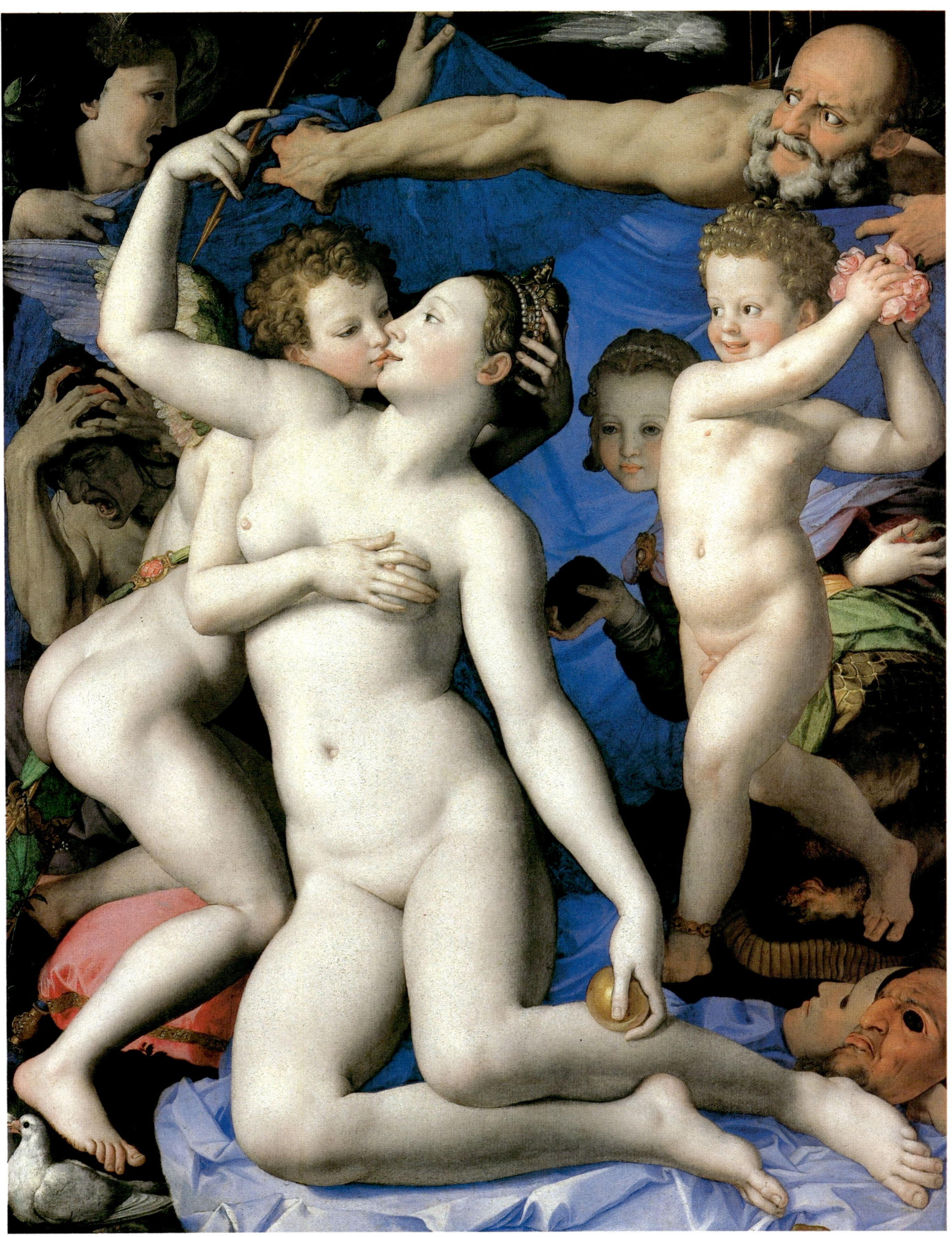

Bernardino Luini, active 1512; died 1532

Christ among the Doctors (No. 18)

Panel, 72.4 × 85.7 cm.
Holwell Carr Bequest 1831

Though the work of Leonardo provided a new stimulus throughout Italy to painters themselves endowed with great originality, in Milan itself his influence imposed a heavier burden on local painters of the early sixteenth century. The most distinguished of these was Bernardino Luini, whose activity is first recorded in 1512, the year after Leonardo's second period of activity in Milan. Luini is best known for his small devotional paintings, usually directly deriving from works by Leonardo, but he also painted, on a more ambitious scale, altarpieces and frescoes which show greater independence of mind, especially in the treatment of narrative and landscape. Many of Luini's paintings, including the *Christ among the Doctors*, have been taken in the past to be originals by Leonardo, and for a brief while in the nineteenth century his own works were regarded by many, Ruskin included, as superior to those of Leonardo, partly because of their more attractive colouring.

The *Christ among the Doctors* was for long a showpiece of the Barberini Gallery in Rome, 'inimitable' according to one eighteenth-century visitor, 'one of the wonderful works of Leonardo da Vinci'. It is indeed securely rooted in Leonardo's art, and may derive from a lost work by Leonardo, who had been asked in 1504 for a picture showing Christ at the age when he confounded the doctors in the Temple. Christ was supposedly twelve years old when this incident took place, but he seems more mature in Luini's panel and he embodies in paint the figure of an ideal other-worldly being which haunted the imagination of Leonardo, appearing in many of his drawings, often juxtaposed with grotesque older men.

Youth and age are similarly contrasted in Luini's painting, Christ gesturing serenely in the foreground, the doctors anxious and consulting together behind him. Though still in argument, Christ is cut off from the doctors, filling the foreground and unnaturally large in scale, and this gives the painting a hieratic and supernatural quality, medieval in its disregard for natural laws. The doctors form a balanced composition to each side of Christ, imbued with the blandness that is endemic to Luini's style, and not unfitted for the part which they play in the story.

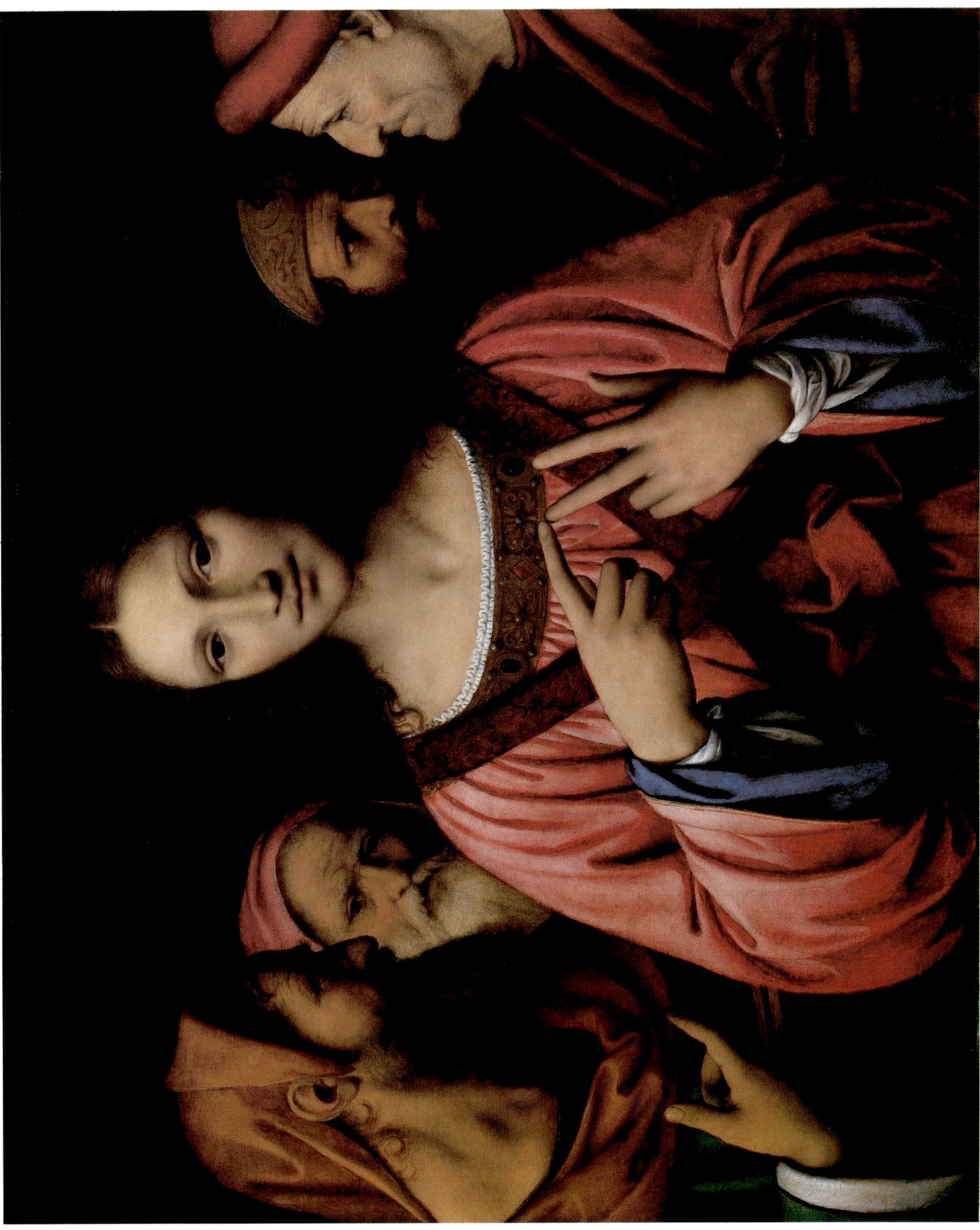

Correggio, active 1514; died 1534

The Madonna of the Basket (No. 23)

Panel, 33.7 × 25.1 cm.
Purchased 1825

The great artists of the school of Parma, Correggio and Parmigianino, who were to make their native town a centre of international importance, created a distinctive local style that profoundly marked the course of painting in the seventeenth century. Antonio Allegri took his name from the town of Correggio, to the east of Parma, where he was born probably between 1489 and 1494. His earliest works show the influence of Mantegna and Costa, painters of the Mantuan court, but in the later 1510s his style was transformed and he began, rather later than his contemporaries in Florence, to discover the work of Leonardo. His two most ambitious works are of the 1520s: the frescoed domes of the church of S. Giovanni Evangelista in Parma and of the Cathedral there.

The Madonna of the Basket, datable to the early 1520s, is one of the smallest of Correggio's paintings, less than a foot wide, yet a work that is not in any way miniaturist in character. In feeling, as in scale, the picture is unusually intimate, the Holy Family shown in a human, though dignified, context. In a misty setting of landscape and architecture S. Joseph is shown at work in the background, while the Virgin, scissors and grey darning wool in the basket beside her, is engaged in the delicate task of putting the baby into his coat. The theme, perhaps suggested by Leonardo's *Yarnwinder Madonna*, is an ingenious invention, touching directly on the poverty of the Holy Family, and alluding more subtly to the events of Christ's Passion: the stripping of his garments; his sacrifice, arms outstretched, on the Cross; and the lamentation itself.

Despite its scale, the figure of the Virgin has a three-dimensional presence not less great than a comparable Virgin in Florentine or Roman painting, and a knowledge of Michelangelo probably lies behind her design. The pose of the child is more complex, the foreshortening recalling Correggio's mastery as a painter of dome frescoes, though its animation is justified by the action of the Virgin. The figures are not, however, in the least sculptural in effect, for Correggio follows Leonardo in his treatment of shadows and in his concentration on feeling. The surfaces are broader and more angular than in Leonardo's painting, and have a greater degree of natural softness. The colours are similarly softened, a homely pinky-brown and blue-green substituted for the usual blue and rose of the Madonna's dress. Submissive and wistfully smiling, Correggio's mother seems the human incarnation of Leonardo's benign but unapproachable Madonnas.

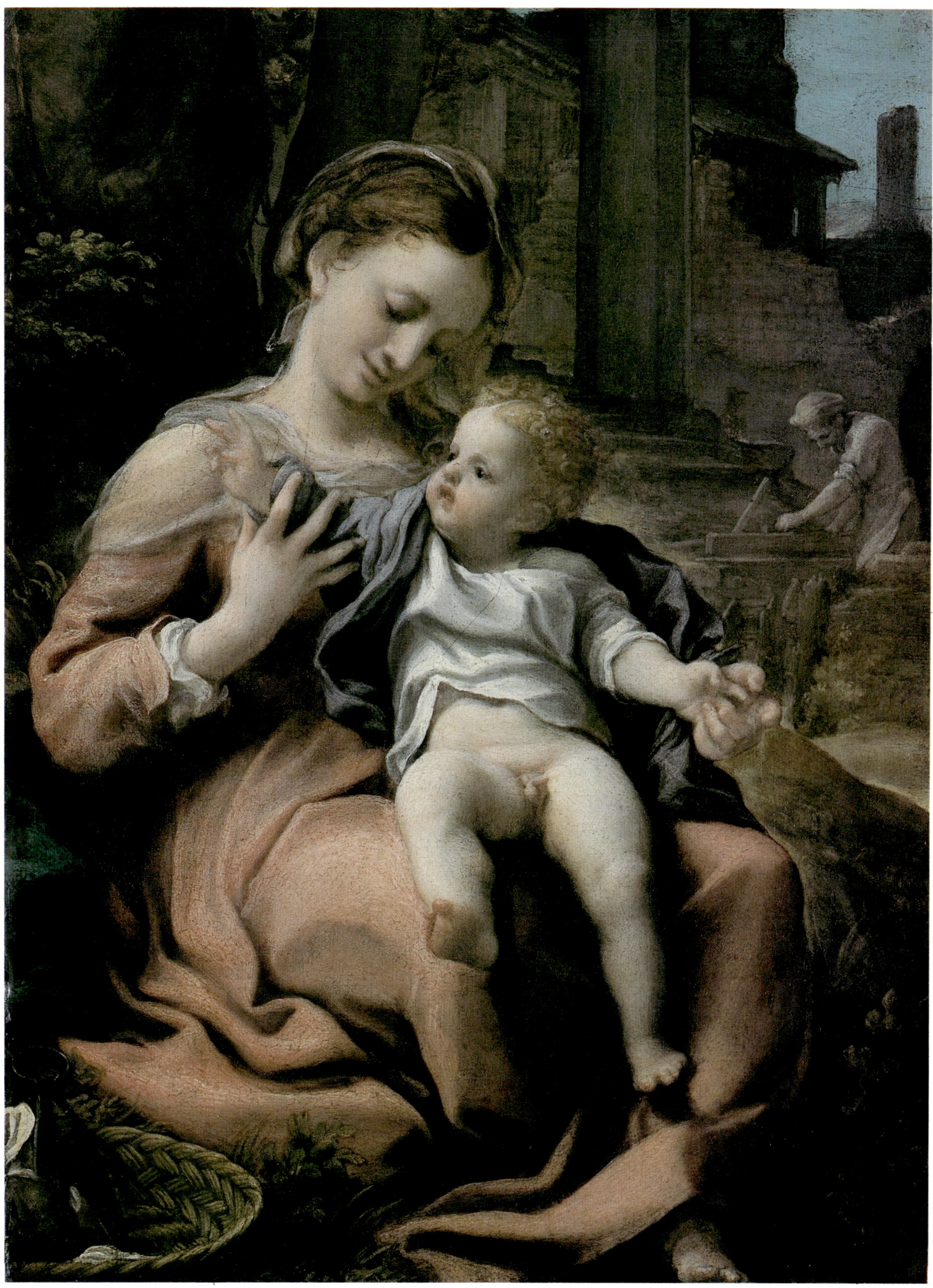

Correggio, active 1514; died 1534

Mercury instructing Cupid before Venus (No. 10)

Canvas, 155.6 × 91.4 cm.
Purchased 1834

Mercury instructing Cupid before Venus is one of the earliest of the mythological paintings produced by Correggio in the later years of his short career, and one whose qualities are not seriously impaired by its damaged condition. Such is the history of this coveted painting that its very survival was frequently in jeopardy. It was painted, probably in the mid-1520s, for the Gonzaga court in Mantua, together with another canvas of similar size, now in the Louvre. Both were acquired with the Mantua collection by King Charles I in 1627. After the Commonwealth sale it travelled to Spain, having been acquired by the Conde-Duque de Olivares, and there it remained until the time of the Peninsular War. It was then carried off by Napoleon's general, Joachim Murat, and removed to Naples. Finally in 1815 the painting was taken to Vienna and sold to a British buyer (Sir Charles Stewart, later Marquess of Londonderry), with whom it returned to London.

The painting is closely akin to *The Madonna of the Basket* (Plate 25) in style and also in the painter's approach to his subject-matter – gods, in this case from the pantheon of antiquity, re-created as humans in spirit and in the flesh, and here, too, inhabiting a darkened wooded landscape, remote from the more conventional Arcadian settings of Venetian and Roman painting. In contrast to the canvas in the Louvre, showing a nude awakening the lust of a satyr, and presumably representing love at its most carnal, the National Gallery painting shows Cupid, the god of love, being instructed in his letters by Mercury. His back with its miniature wings is turned towards his mother and his attention concentrated on the paper which Mercury lowers for his inspection.

Venus, who is unusual in having wings, has the piquant and unclassical features common to all Correggio's heroines, but her pose is rooted in classical art, like that of Raphael's *S. Catherine* (Plate 8), and it, too, may have been suggested by the lost *Leda* by Leonardo. It was not without difficulty, however, that the postures of the figures were established by the painter, and X-ray photographs show many differences from the composition as it finally appeared. Like Venus, the figures of Mercury and Cupid probably also derive from a classical source, a sculpture in relief, but master and pupil are transformed and domesticated by the painter, the tenderness of their relationship conveyed by the popular, if misleading, title '*The School of Love*'.

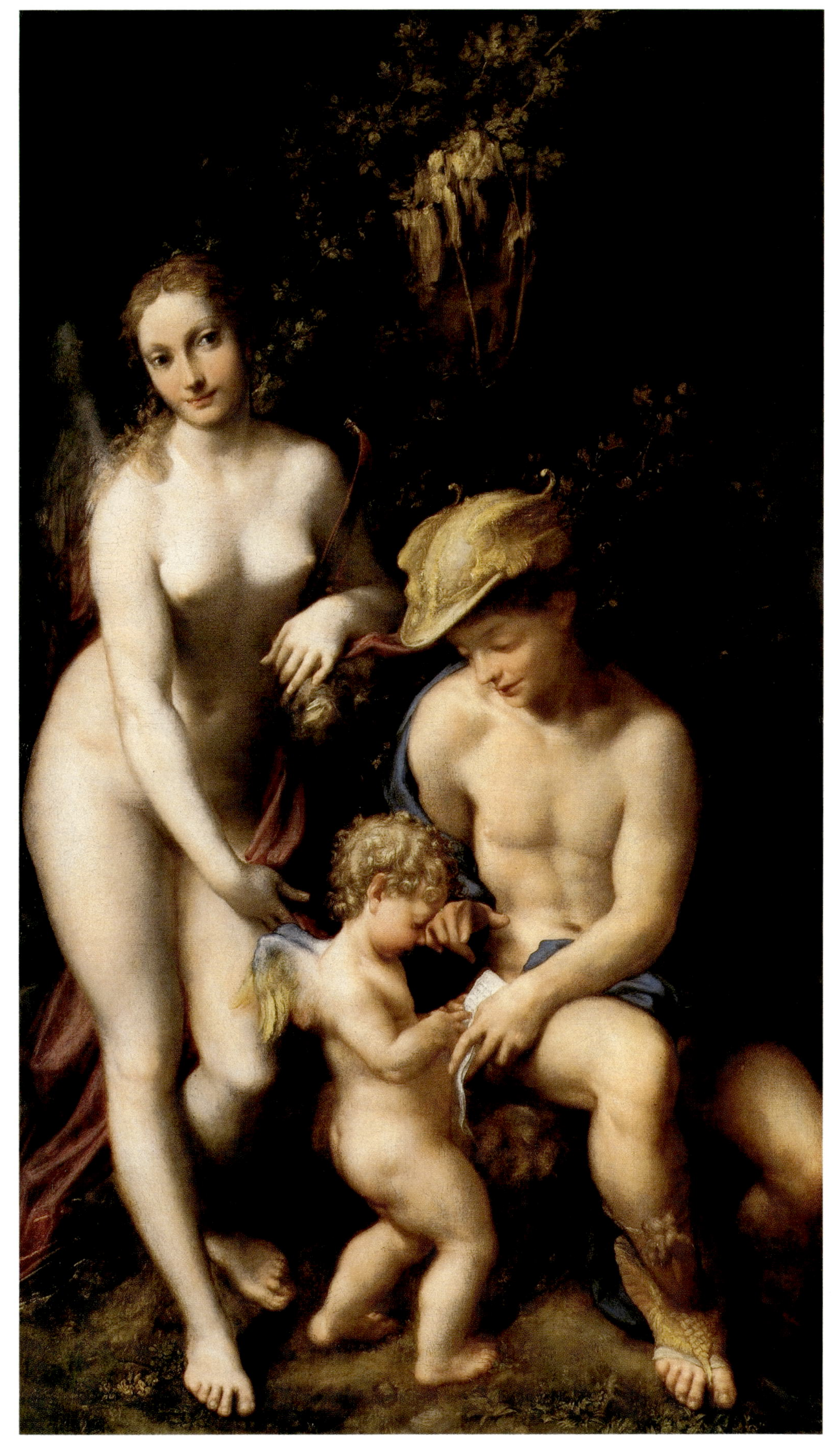

Parmigianino, 1503–1540

Altarpiece : Madonna and Child with SS. John the Baptist and Jerome (No. 33)

Panel, 353 × 149 cm.
Presented by the Governors of the British Institution 1826

Born in Parma, Parmigianino was a painter deeply influenced by Correggio, though more precocious and impressionable than the older artist. He travelled in 1524 to Rome, where he remained until the sack of the city by a band of northern troops in 1527. Like other painters attracted by the capital in the wake of Raphael and Michelangelo, he then sought refuge in the north, moving to Bologna before returning to his native town.

Vasari, his first biographer, described his obsession with alchemy in the later years of his short life, a passion not unrelated to the intense and experimental nature of his art, which led to his virtual abandonment of painting before his death at Casalmaggiore, near Parma, in 1540. His style, though based in origin on that of Correggio, developed towards a far greater sophistication and conscious elegance, influenced by his experience of Rome, an alchemy of 'naturalism' and artifice as haunting in its very different way as the art of Leonardo.

The *Madonna and Child with SS. John the Baptist and Jerome*, carried out in Rome in 1527, is easily the largest, apart from Parmigianino's works in fresco, and one of the most important of his surviving paintings. Its elongated shape, determined by the architecture of the chapel in which it was to be placed, is in accordance with the exaggerated proportions of the figures within the painting, which reflect Michelangelo's canon for the human body as developed in the 1520s. The setting, with its lush and feathery vegetation, freely painted in shades of brilliant green, is derived from the work of Correggio, confirming Vasari's high estimate of the painter's feeling for landscape. From Correggio, too, comes the figure of S. Jerome, sketched as broadly in paint as the grassy bank on which he lies asleep. Correggio had introduced a sleeping saint (S. Roch) in a late altarpiece (now in Dresden), and in Parmigianino's altarpiece he serves to underline the visionary character of the theme.

In contrast to the figure of S. Jerome is the energetic S. John, who dominates the foreground of the painting. As in Raphael's *Ansidei Madonna* (Plate 6), it is he who directs attention to the Virgin and Child, but this is a being of a different order. Recalling Leonardo's painting of the Baptist (Louvre, Paris), he fixes the spectator with a warning stare and stretches out across the painting in a pose of exaggerated contortion, pointing upwards with a hooked and elongated finger.

The barrier between the real and the painted world had been frequently disturbed in fresco paintings, and Parmigianino was here one of the first painters to attempt such an experiment in an altarpiece. The foot of S. John is level with the edge of the painting, so that his knee and his arm are thrust forward beyond the picture plane, illuminated by the light that fell across the chapel where the painting was to be installed. By this means the brilliant vision in the sky above, the chief glory of the painting, is ushered into prominence with an immediacy that cannot be ignored.

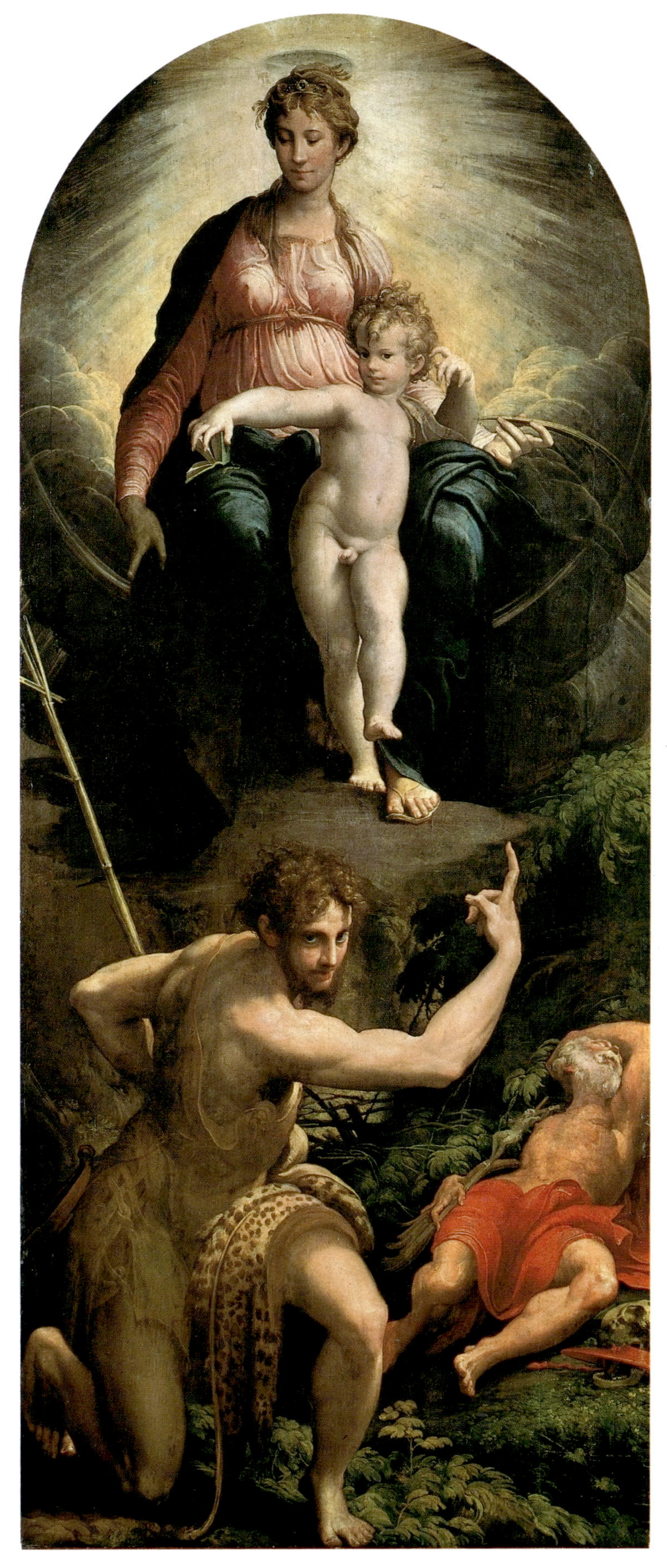

Parmigianino, 1503–1540

Altarpiece, detail of Plate 27

Vasari implies that Parmigianino was working on the *Madonna and Child with SS. John the Baptist and Jerome* when the sack of Rome took place. 'Having then been commissioned to paint for Madonna Maria Bufolini of Città di Castello a panel picture which was to be placed in S. Salvatore del Lauro in a chapel near the door, Francesco painted in it a Madonna in the sky, who is reading and has the Child between her knees, and on the earth a figure of S. John. . . . But he was prevented from bringing this work to completion by the ruin and sack of Rome in 1527, which was the reason not only that the arts were banished for a time, but also that many craftsmen lost their lives. And Francesco, also, came within a hair's breadth of losing his, seeing that at the beginning of the sack he was so intent on his work that, when the soldiers were entering the houses, and some Germans were already in his, he did not move from his painting for all the uproar they were making; but when they came upon him and saw him working they were so struck with astonishment at the work that, like the gentlemen that they must have been, they let him go on.'

No doubt the story was exaggerated by Vasari, although the obsessive character of the painter is not discordant with his evidence, and the figure of S. John may have been finished in some haste. The upper part of the painting is in contrast immaculate in appearance, and imbued with a conscious elegance that anticipates the style of Bronzino (Plate 23). The miraculous character of the vision is conveyed by its more studied handling, the elaborated beauty and something also of the repose of antique sculpture serving in a new way to convey the message of the Christian faith. The golden hair of the Madonna is arranged in burnished curls and loops about her head, and her dress creates an equally complex pattern as it falls across her body and arms. With eyes downcast she holds in her left hand what may be a quill, though it also resembles a martyr's palm, and directs attention towards the Child grasping the book upon her lap and to the elongated cross of S. John which projects into the upper part of the painting. The Child himself has in contrast the lively presence and almost coy appeal that remained peculiar to the painter's portrayals of children.

The disposition of the figures recalls the work of Michelangelo – his early group of the Madonna and Child in Bruges, as well as the more elongated proportions of his figures of the 1520s. The two halves of the painting, though they differ in treatment, are not, however, discordant. The Child is posed in relation to the figure of S. John, the limbs of the two figures forging a strong central axis of the painting, and their prominent gestures matching in reverse. The sombre shadows of the landscape merge with the clouds in the upper part of the painting and the auriole of grey that enhances the statuesque Madonna, presiding in thought over the scene enacted in her presence.

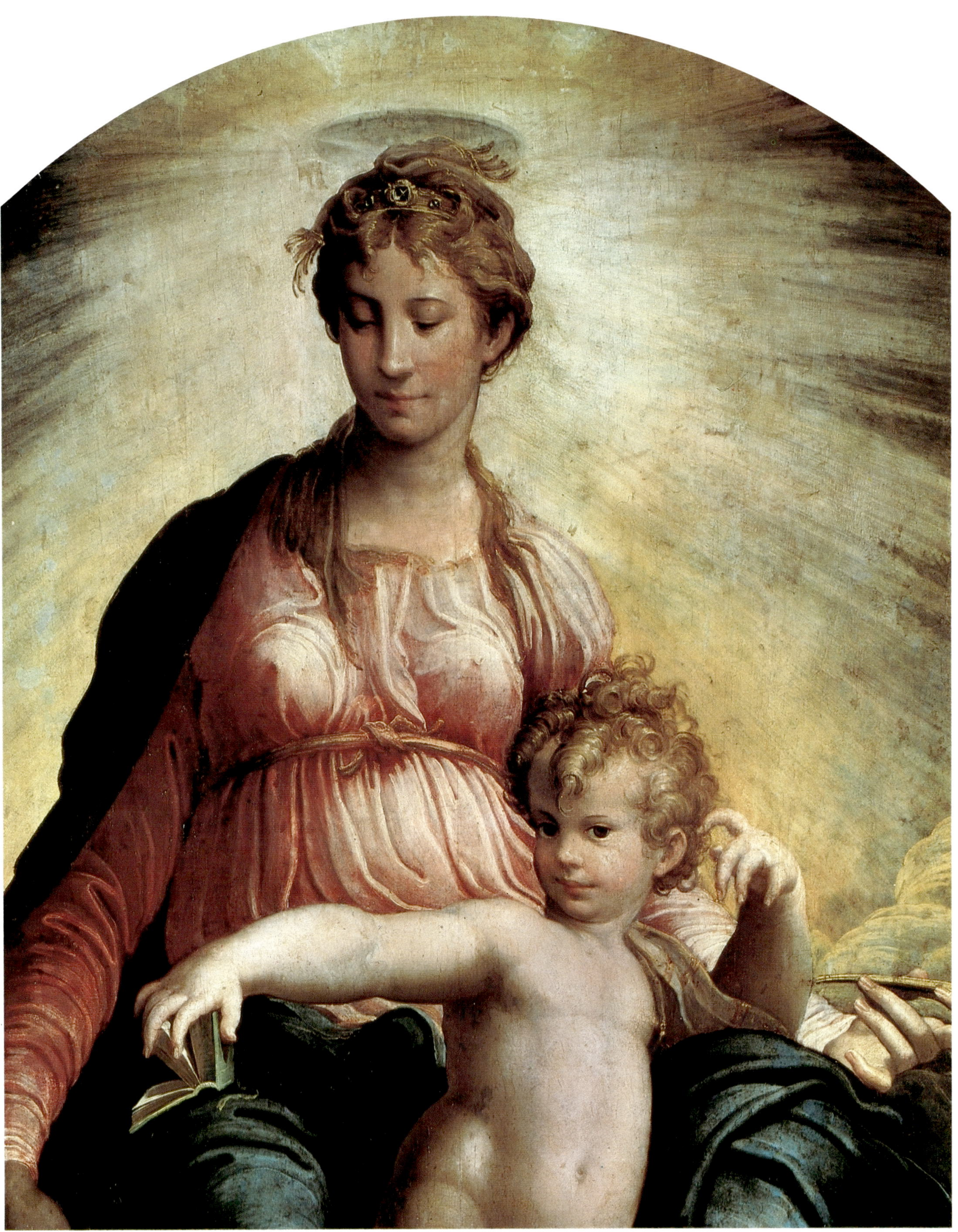

Parmigianino, 1503–1540

The Mystic Marriage of S. Catherine (No. 6427)

Panel, 74.2 × 57.2 cm.
Purchased 1974

As the progress of painting in Italy in the early years of the sixteenth century increasingly affected the art of northern Europe (the elegance of Parmigianino's art later making its own distinct contribution to this development), so, too, Italian painters became aware of the achievements of painters in the north. As well as the exploration of oil paint as a medium, which is taken to an extreme of delicacy and freedom in many of the works of Parmigianino, there was in northern Europe a hierarchy of values that excluded no part of the visible world as a fit subject for paintings, even in religious art. Scenes of the Holy Family in domestic interiors, sometimes on a small scale, became a feature of painting in Rome in the 1520s amongst the followers of Raphael, and it is in this context that Parmigianino's *Mystic Marriage of S. Catherine* has its own special significance.

S. Catherine of Alexandria, a princess of Egypt, who had been shown by Raphael (Plate 8) almost like a goddess of the classical past, is presented here by Parmigianino as an actress in a more domestic idyll. She had seen in a vision the Madonna and the Child, who had turned towards her and later placed a ring upon her finger symbolizing her marriage to God. Spiritual betrothal was the significance of the subject, and this was presumably the meaning that Parmigianino's patron attached to the commission, contributing to the form in which the painter cast his image. It may have been painted before the artist left Rome, or in the time immediately following, when he fled to Bologna.

The placing of the ring is the focus of the painting, S. Catherine offering a delicate hand to the Child, while her left arm rests upon the spiked wheel that is her normal attribute. A green curtain gives emphasis to the saint, setting off the elaborate beauty of her hair adorned with a jewelled tiara, while the subdued red of her skirt adds a discreet suggestion of warmth to this side of the painting. Eclipsed in physical beauty by S. Catherine, the Virgin turns her body into the painting and her hair is covered by a scarf. This intensifies the domestic character of the scene, but the Child looks up to his mother as he places the ring on S. Catherine's finger, and in this way the authority of the Virgin is not seriously diminished.

The scene is witnessed by two figures who appear in the doorway in the background. Normally the mother of the Virgin, S. Anne, and Joseph are additional figures present in paintings of the subject, but S. Joseph's is presumably the haloed head in the foreground. Curiously removed from the scene of action, he mediates like S. John (Plate 27) between the spectator and the vision beyond, and directs attention across the foreground towards the wheel of S. Catherine.

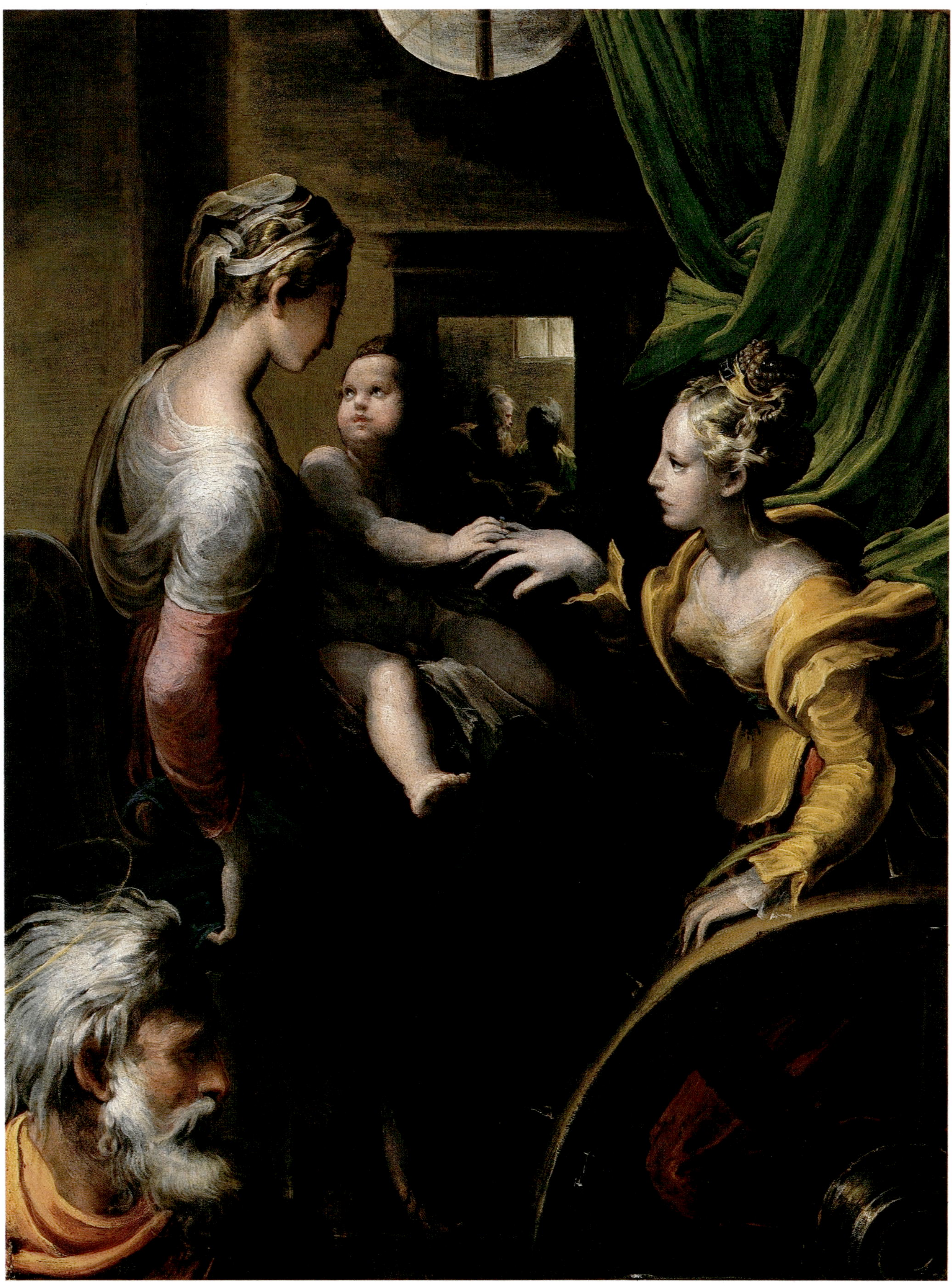

Parmigianino, 1503–1540

Portrait of a Collector (No. 6441)

Panel, 89.5 × 63.8 cm.
Purchased 1977

Parmigianino was judged by Vasari as a painter who excelled Correggio 'in grace, adornment and beauty of manner', but 'even as there is a perfect illusion of the sight', he added, 'so there is present the beating of the pulse, according as it but pleased his brush'. The more naturalistic side of Parmigianino's art, 'the beating of the pulse', is exemplified in his accomplished and often peculiarly intense portraits, beginning with a celebrated *Self-portrait* (Vienna), which he painted before the age of twenty on a round convex panel in imitation of a likeness in a mirror.

The *Portrait of a Collector* was in the Farnese collection in Parma in the seventeenth century and it is usually considered a painting that Parmigianino carried out before he left his native city in 1524. Precocious though the painter may have been, a portrait of such authority and psychological penetration could scarcely be the work of so young an artist, whose paintings are often too experimental in character to be very easily datable. More than Raphael, or Titian, or Sarto (Plates 9, 14 and 20), Parmigianino shows himself alive to the disconcerting presence of a far from affable sitter. The darkly shadowed eyes look sideways and downwards beneath frowning brows and a high forehead partly covered by a dark hat and matted hair. From this brooding and memorable focus all the other parts of the composition derive their placing and a curiously heightened significance.

Nature and art are juxtaposed at the level of the head where a narrow opening on the right aligned with the hat shows a dark and freely painted landscape. A broken classical relief, echoing the shape of the hat, appears to the left, as though forming part of the sitter's collection. Venus and Mars with Cupid seems to be the subject of the sculpture, a scene of domestic felicity that is brightly illuminated from the background where the rising, or more probably the setting, sun competes with a menacing sky.

As though directly exposed to the elements the sitter wears a coat lined with fur, and he holds what is probably a book in a chased and jewelled binding. The other arm rests upon the table, which serves in place of a parapet in the foreground of the painting. Here a metal statuette and four coins, one showing the head of a classical emperor, are placed casually across its patterned border. The hand and its elegant fingers seem as much on display as the other objects upon the table, straying not far away and ready to remove them again from sight. The possessions seem not sufficiently plentiful truly to justify the title of the painting, though the image is one of the most haunting expressions in portraiture of the melancholic temperament, suggesting a lonely and obsessive existence, like the life of the painter himself in his declining years.

Niccolò dell'Abate, born about 1509–12; died 1571

The Story of Aristaeus   (No. 5283)

Canvas, 188 × 237 cm.
Presented by the National Art-Collections Fund 1941

The Story of Aristaeus is a canvas painted probably not in Italy, but in France, where Niccolò dell'Abate passed most of his later life. He was born in Modena, and his earliest works – principally fresco decorations – were carried out there and in Bologna. He was deeply affected by the work of Parmigianino, and Dosso Dossi (Plate 37) is claimed as an influence on his landscapes. The painting of landscape was, however, a comparatively recent development, associated less with Italy than with northern art, and it was only after his arrival in France in 1552 that Niccolò became an early and distinguished exponent.

From the very beginning of the sixteenth century, the French court had looked with envy upon the achievements of Italian civilization, and during the reign of Francis I (1515–1547) several outstanding Italian painters (including Leonardo) had been lured to France. In the 1530s the Tuscan painter Rosso Fiorentino, and Primaticcio, a native of Bologna who had worked with Raphael's pupil Giulio Romano in Mantua, were employed at the palace of Fontainebleau, where they created a new style of decoration, combining painting with sculpture, that transformed the course of art in northern Europe. After Rosso's early death, Primaticcio took on the leading role at Fontainebleau, and it was in association with him that Niccolò worked after his arrival in France.

The decorative purpose of *The Story of Aristaeus* is manifested in its scale and in the elaboration of the landscape, an undulating coastal fantasy pictured from a high viewpoint, which is related in style and in its relatively subdued colouring to the work, generally on a smaller scale, of the Antwerp school of so-called 'Mannerist' landscape painters. The obscure and fantastic story illustrated by the painting is little more than the pretext for the landscape, though the actions of the figures in the foreground with their wildly fluttering draperies are distantly mirrored in the insubstantial clouds that are blown across the sky.

Virgil in the *Georgics* (IV, 315–558) describes how the shepherd Aristaeus, concerned about the death of his bees, consulted his mother, Cyrene, who advised him to speak to the sea-god, Proteus. He learnt that he was being punished by Orpheus because Eurydice had been bitten by a serpent while being chased by Aristaeus, and so had gone to the underworld. The chase is shown in the centre of the painting with Eurydice stepping on the serpent, and on the right she lies dead. The river-god on the far right is probably Proteus, and the figures above him most likely Aristaeus and his mother. In the background the mourning Orpheus plays his lyre, surrounded by animals, including a unicorn, which have emerged from the forest to hear the music.

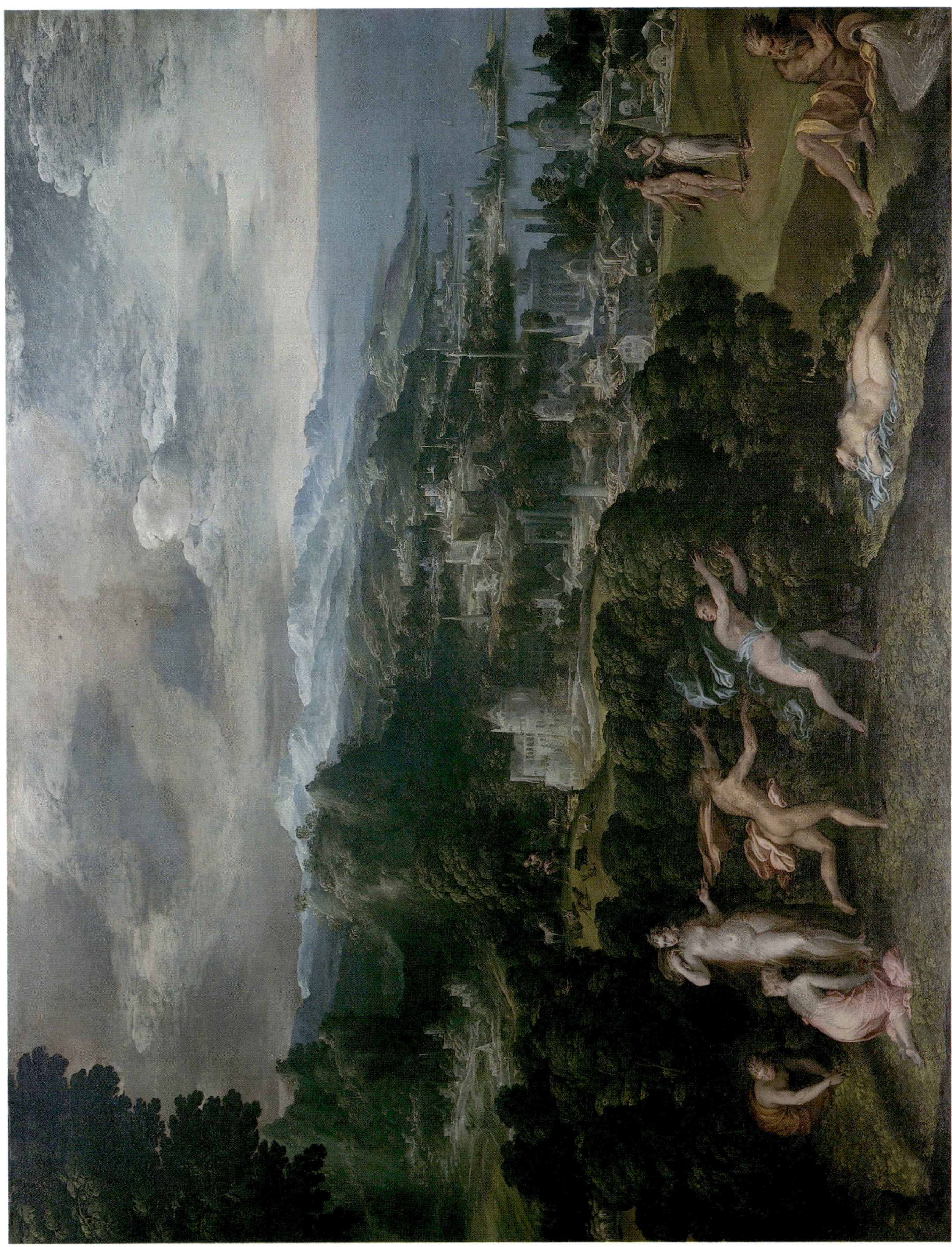

Gerolamo Romanino, born about 1484–87; died 1562(?)

S. Alessandro (panel from an altarpiece) (No. 297)

Panel, 158.8 × 64.8 cm.
Purchased 1857

From Venice the influence of Giorgione and Titian spread throughout a large part of northern Italy, which had come under the political control of Venice in the early sixteenth century. While Milan, Parma and Bologna remained independent of Venice, Milan itself becoming a Spanish province, Brescia and Bergamo, not many miles away, were the western outposts of the Venetian empire. Local artistic traditions in these areas – a receptiveness to northern painting and the 'naturalism' associated with this part of Lombardy – reacted to the new style of Venice with lively and varied results.

Romanino was a native of Brescia, though active over a wide area of northern Italy, and in 1559 he became a municipal councillor of his native town. His *S. Alessandro*, one of the most Venetian of his works, is one panel of an altarpiece in the National Gallery painted probably around 1525 for the church of S. Alessandro in Brescia. The warrior saint stands in the place of honour beside the central panel, which shows the Nativity of Christ. He is matched by a full-length S. Jerome, contrasted in age and dress, and the two saints represent the active and the contemplative aspects of the central Christian mystery. The altarpiece corresponds in its compartmented character with one painted by Titian in 1522 for the church of SS. Nazaro and Celso in Brescia, showing the Resurrection in the centre. The old-fashioned polyptych form persisted in parts of northern Italy, especially with narratives with which the accompanying saints had no direct historical connection.

As befits the titular saint of the church, standing in the place of honour, S. Alessandro is much the grandest figure in the altarpiece. Seen from below in statuesque pose, with one knee projecting forwards, he bears a lance draped with a rose-coloured flag striped with pink which is looped across his back. The rich pigmentation of the figure, the fawn and green of his dress carrying up into the sky the colours of the landscape, is Venetian in effect, though the handling of the paint has a roughness, more apparent in other works by Romanino, which contributes to the liveliness if not to the elegance of the image. With pronounced emphasis the saint, whose helmet lies on the ground at his feet, turns to gaze down towards the central panel of the altar, where the viewpoint is lower, the Child lying in the manger with the Virgin in prayer before him.

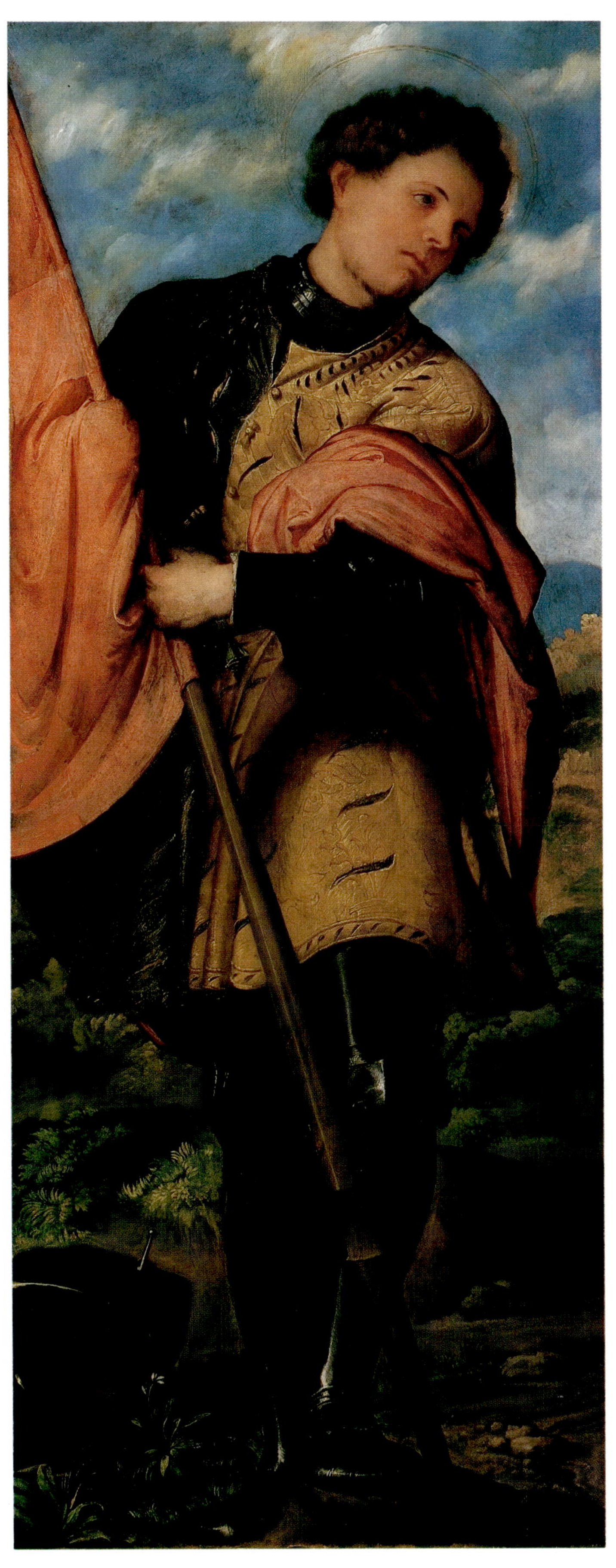

Moretto da Brescia, born about 1498; died 1554

Portrait of a Gentleman (No. 1025)

Dated: . M . D . XXVI
Canvas, 201.3 × 92.1 cm.
Purchased 1876

Alessandro Bonvicino, called Moretto da Brescia, was some fifteen years younger than Romanino. Working mainly in his native town, he was extensively employed, like Romanino, by the Church, but he was also gifted in portraiture, passing on this skill to his pupil Moroni (Plates 49 and 50). He is indeed distinguished from Romanino by a style that is more literal in its description of natural appearances, his paint more carefully applied and curiously flattening in its effect, colouring that is rarely other than sombre, and an attention to detail that creates, in some of his religious narratives, an almost Victorian sense of physical actuality.

The *Portrait of a Gentleman*, bearing in prominent Roman numerals the date 1526, has the distinction of being (as far as is known) the first of an important series of full-length, life-size portraits produced in northern Italy in the sixteenth century. This was a phenomenon related more to northern art than to the Renaissance tradition in Italy even in its later development, when, for example, the portraits of Bronzino, painted on panel rather than on canvas, never exceeded half-length scale. The painting was purchased for the National Gallery as one of a group of four portraits from the Avogadro–Fenaroli collection in Brescia, and the sitter may be Gerolamo Avogadro, the father of the man portrayed by Moroni (Plate 49) in a later full-length that derives from Moretto's composition.

The presentation of the upper half of the figure by Moretto recalls the early portraits of Titian in the amplitude of the silhouette, which contrasts here with the diminutive size of the ungloved hand. The sitter turns to gaze reflectively into the distance and his hat, the strongest note of colour in the painting, is decorated with a prominent S. Christopher badge.

The elbow and leg to the left, both clothed in brown, project in the same direction as the glance, the puffed sleeve and wide-toed shoes showing how fashions themselves responded to the visual priorities of the early years of the century. To broaden still further the silhouette, the cloak is spread out on the plinth of a giant column. The architecture, projecting above the sitter's head but with parallel lines of staining creating a horizontal stress at the top of the canvas, was perhaps suggested to Moretto by an earlier narrative or religious composition. It is used to define in some detail the pose of the sitter, and equally its presence confers on him a borrowed grandeur, a device by which no later portrait specialist remained unaffected.

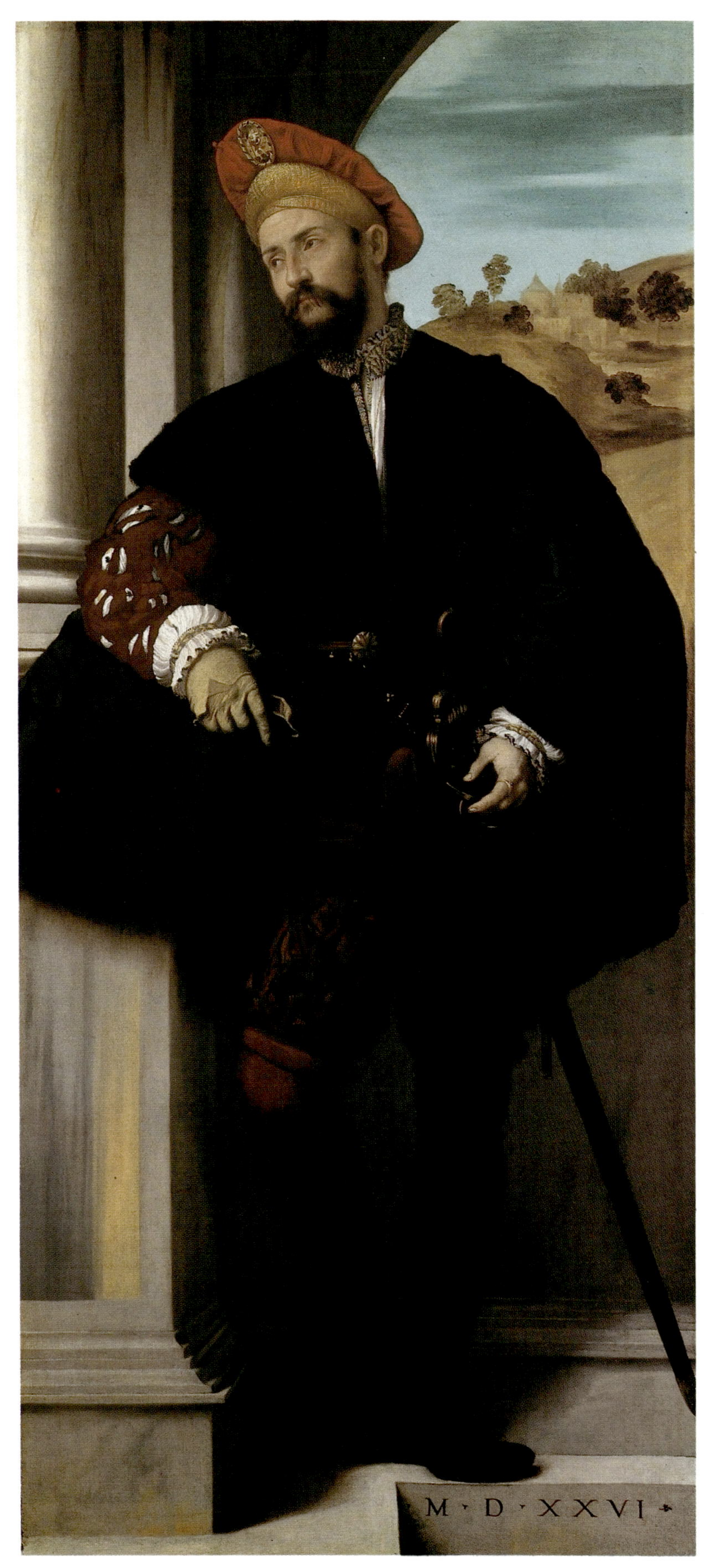

M · D · XXVI ·

Gian Girolamo Savoldo, active 1508; died after 1548

S. Mary Magdalen approaching the Sepulchre (No. 1031)

Canvas, 86.4 × 79.4 cm.
Purchased 1878

Brescia was the birthplace of Gian Girolamo Savoldo, but his working life was spent for the most part in Venice, where his presence is documented from 1521 to 1548. He painted mainly religious themes and, of the relatively few canvases that are known, many are repetitions of the same compositions. Not a prolific or successful artist, he was, however, famous as a pioneer in the painting of night scenes.

Indicating an overriding affection for Savoldo's adopted town are the views of Venice which figure in the backgrounds of many of his paintings, even when the theme is scarcely apposite (as, for example, the *Rest on the Flight into Egypt*). This is one element of the general strangeness of Savoldo's artistic personality, which also shows itself in a disregard for accepted standards of sophistication and elegance. Though not un-Venetian in their breadth and in colour, Savoldo's paintings hint at the revolution in values that Caravaggio brought to Italian painting in the very last years of the century.

The *S. Mary Magdalen approaching the Sepulchre* is a version, perhaps of about 1530, of one of Savoldo's more Titianesque compositions. Muffled in a cloak of shimmering grey (a colour that resembles the lilac of mourning) the saint stands beside the half-open sepulchre, where her vase is placed. She appears to draw back rather than approach the tomb, sensing the miracle of the Resurrection and turning directly to the sepulchre with upraised arm beneath her cloak. Dawn rises in the background over the city of Venice, lighting up the clouds and a sky already intensely blue. The dignity of the subject seems well matched to the grave and inert style of the painter, and to his preoccupation with unusual lighting effects.

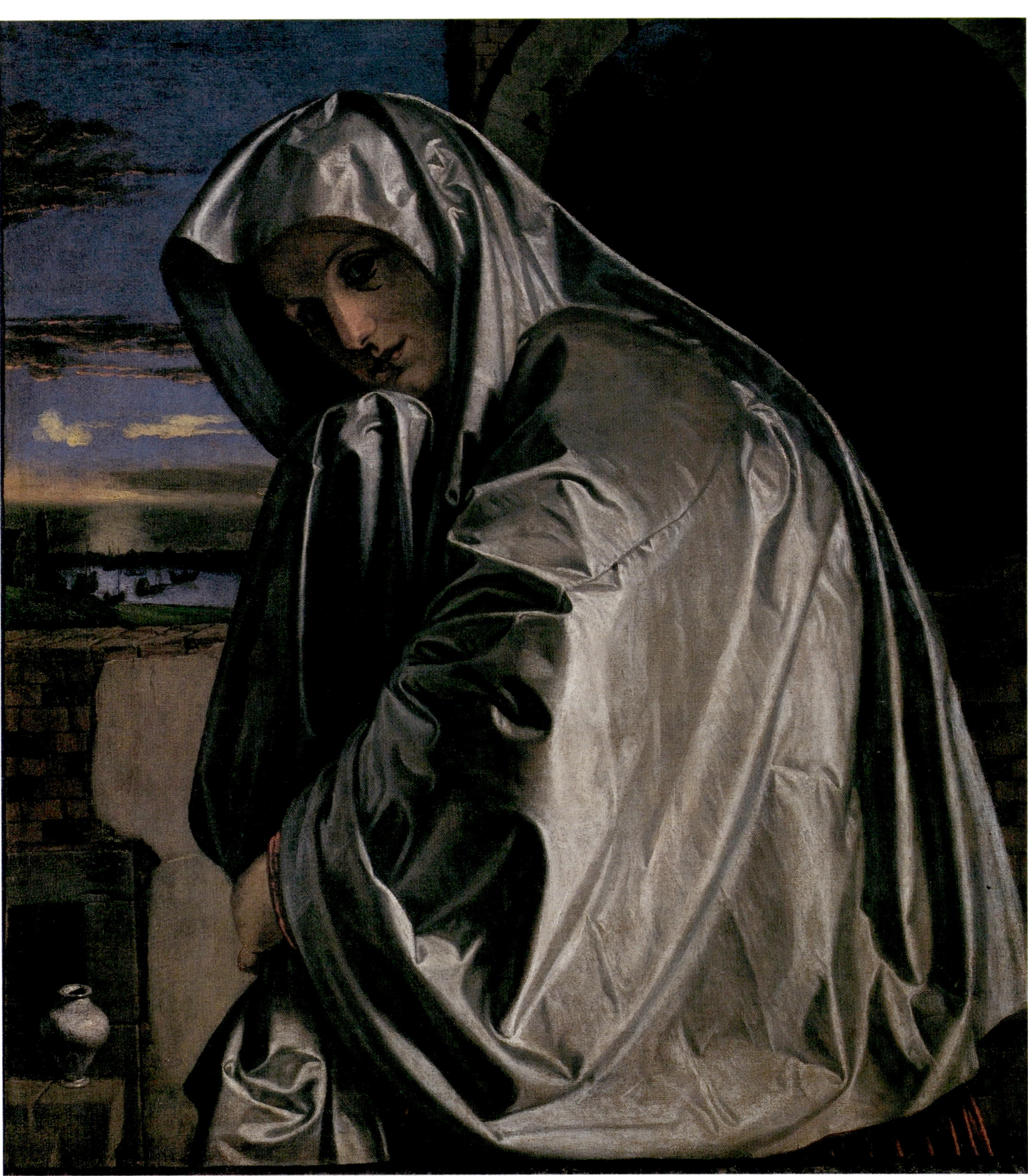

Lorenzo Lotto, born about 1480; died 1556/7

Portrait of a Lady   (No. 4256)

Inscribed (on the paper): NEC VLLA IMPUDICA LV / CRETIAE EXEMPLO VIVET
Canvas, 95.9 × 110.5 cm.
Purchased 1927

Venice was probably the birthplace of Lotto, and where he received his early training, but he was later active over a wide area of northern Italy, including Bergamo (1523–35) and the Marches. He moved in his old age to Loreto, and attached himself to the service of the church of the Santa Casa there. The restlessness of his journeying, which is documented in an account book (a rare survival) from the later part of his life, is not unrelated to the disturbing character of his art. His experience of Venetian art was of fundamental importance, though in colouring his approach is notably experimental and provocative. The expressive character of German art also held an appeal for him, and he found some equivalent to this in the lively frescoes of Correggio.

Like many other north Italian and Venetian painters he excelled in portraiture, especially with Lotto when the sitter could be shown actively engaged, and for such portraits he frequently employed 'landscape'-shaped canvases more commonly associated in Venice with religious compositions. Many of these paintings show Lotto as the outstanding exponent of allegorical portraiture, where the artist was busied with inventing details symbolic of the sitters and their states of mind.

In the *Portrait of a Lady* the sitter points to a drawing of Lucretia, who is shown with dagger in hand about to kill herself after being ravished by Tarquin. Symbolizing virtue, the drawing is held at arm's length over a table where an unfolded paper with an inscription is laid out and a nosegay of flowers. The wording of the inscription, turned into a verse couplet, is from Livy (*History*, I): NEC VLLA IMPUDICA LV / CRETIAE EXEMPLO VIVET ('after Lucretia's example let no unchaste woman live').

The portrait was in the Pesaro collection in Venice and the lady is probably Lucrezia Valier who married Benedetto Pesaro in 1533. It would date from about this time, and given the insistence in the portrait on the chastity of the sitter it may well be a marriage portrait, foreign to modern eyes in its elaborate protestation of virtue but not discordant with the more boastful priorities of the sixteenth century. Even the clothes of the sitter are unusually showy – her dress of striped orange and green, with a grey fur lining that matches the colour of the background, her fashionably dressed and ribboned hair, and her jewelled necklace which is given especial prominence, tucked into the neck of her dress. Contrasting with the colours of the dress is the mulberry-coloured tablecloth, which gives emphasis on the right to the symbols of her virtue.

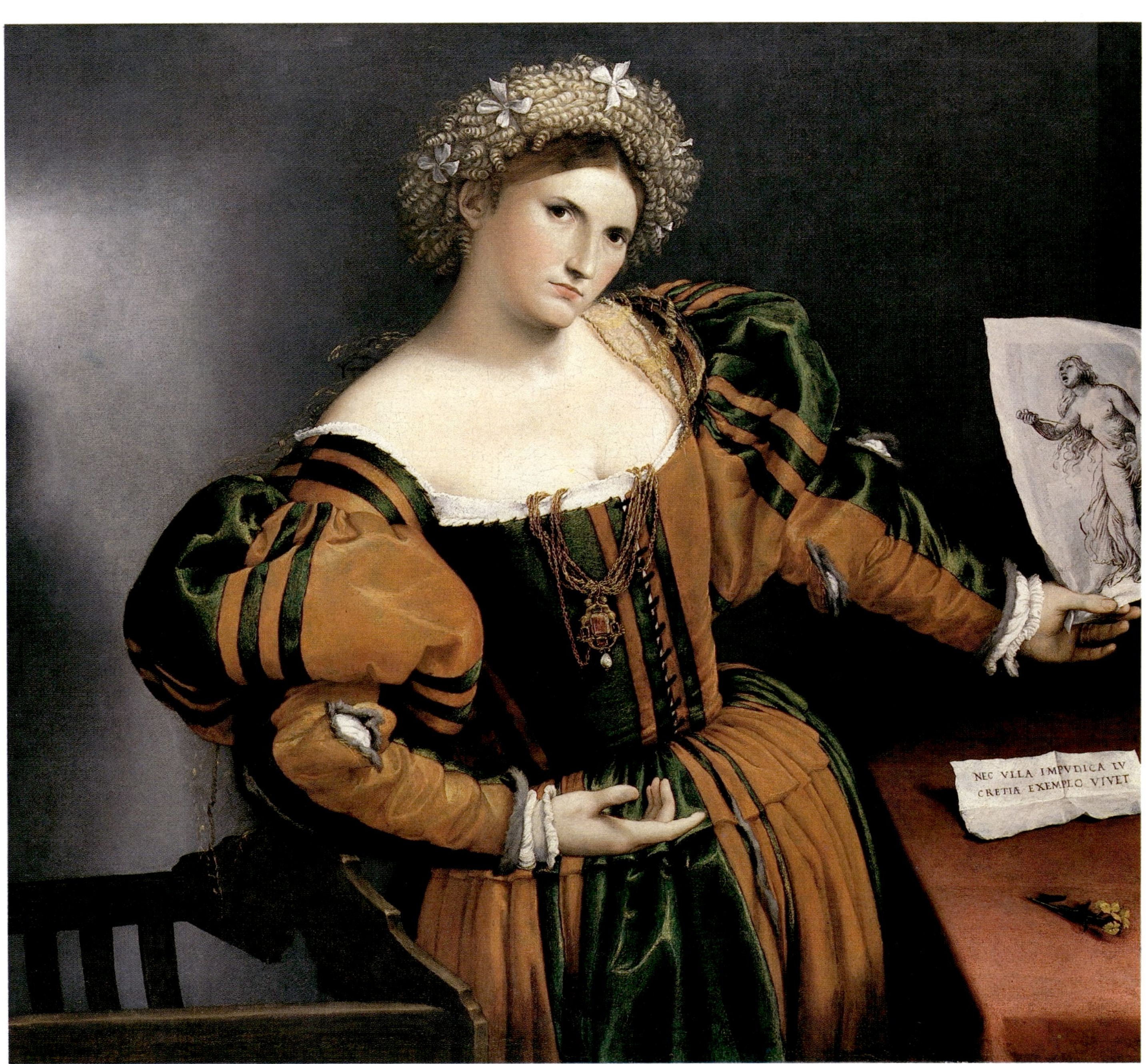

NEC VLLA IMPVDICA LV
CRETIA EXEMPLO VIVET

Lorenzo Lotto, born about 1480; died 1556/7

Family Group (No. 1047)

Signed, upper right: . L. Lotto
Canvas, 114.9 × 139.7 cm.
Bequeathed by Miss Sarah Solly 1879

Lotto's *Family Group* has been connected with an entry in his account book on 23 September 1547 which refers to a portrait of a Giovanni della Volta ('Zuane de la Volta') with his wife and two children, 'judged for quality and the finest colours' at the value of fifty ducats. As the painting is the only known portrait by Lotto of a family group with two children, and as a dating in the later 1540s appears probable, the identification of the family is likely to be correct.

Inevitably, Lotto in his portrait conveys much of the liveliness of family life, even with parents who seem so inherently sober in demeanour, looking directly from the painting with unaffected severity. No doubt the bowl of cherries upon the table and the action to which it gives rise has a significance, beyond its mere presence as a treat, which is no longer accessible to interpretation. Dressed only in a transparent veil, the child below the table is shown to be male, and he stretches upwards to receive a pair of cherries from his father, guided from behind by the father's protecting hand. His sister sits on the table to the left, helping herself from the bowl and from her mother's hand.

Both parents incline into the painting, towards their children, and opening beyond their heads is a prospect of distant landscape, where a smoking volcano (referring less to Venice than to Naples) is shown beside a bleak expanse of sea and sky. The 'finest colours' are confined to the foreground, where rose and blue are the predominant tones and the forms, especially noticeable in the hands, have the curiously flattened appearance that is common to many of Lotto's later works, distantly anticipating the latest style of Rembrandt. Richer in colour and in incident than the landscape is the striking Turkish carpet of orange, red and gold, with its green and white border, that covers the table in front of the window. This is of a type, imported from overseas by sixteenth-century Italian merchants, that has come to be known as a 'Lotto' carpet because so frequently used by the painter in his compositions.

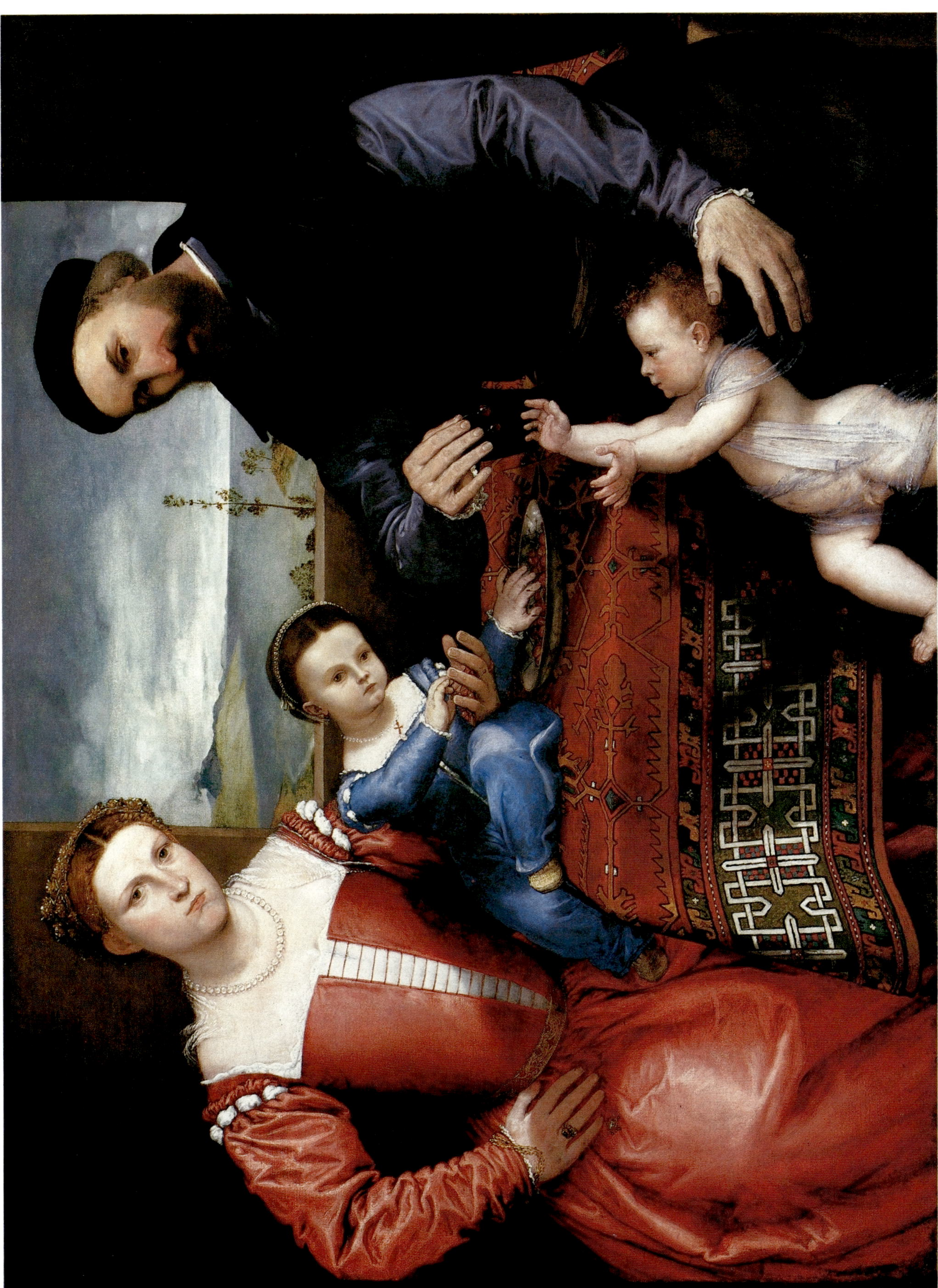

Dosso Dossi, active 1512; died 1542

The Adoration of the Kings (No. 3924)

Panel, 85.1 × 108 cm.
Mond Bequest 1924

The feeling shown by painters active in north Italy, and especially by Lotto, for emotional expressiveness and complex allegory was to a large extent shared by the Ferrarese painter Dosso Dossi, but in Dosso's greatest paintings an overriding respect for the personal achievement of Giorgione is apparent. From these different elements, overlaid in later works by the influence of Raphael and Michelangelo, an uneven and eccentric style emerged, rising at times to rival the poetic intensity of the greatest Venetian art. Little is known of Dosso's personal life; he is first recorded in Mantua and then from 1514 until his death as court painter in Ferrara, where he was chiefly active in the decoration of the castle, contributing works to the room for which Titian's *Bacchus and Ariadne* (Plate 15) was painted.

The Adoration of the Kings, which may be a painting of the 1520s or later, is one of Dosso's most vibrant and Giorgionesque creations – the story of the Adoration of the Kings re-enacted in an enchanted setting that might seem more suited to the scenes of magic and sorcery in the *Orlando* of Ariosto (Plate 17). The landscape is illuminated by a moon of portentous size, partly veiled in cloud and visible through the glowing foliage of a tree.

So free is the brushwork that its light appears to flicker across the landscape from the village with its church in the distance towards the brightly clad figures in the front. Illuminated mysteriously from a hidden source of light in the foreground, their clothes punctuate the surface of the painting with areas of brilliant colour that are contrasted with the shadows of the foliage behind.

The Holy Family is placed to the left outside a roofed shelter where two figures are glimpsed in the darkness. The Virgin looks down at two of the kings kneeling in the shadow at her feet, and gestures towards the landscape. S. Joseph to the left reclines upon the ground, the lower corner of a pyramid of which the apex is formed by the Madonna and Child. Rose and blue and green are the colours to each side of the composition, interrupted in the centre by the golden cloak of the second king, wrapped closely about his body and creating a hiatus between the landscape and the main figure group. The space to the right is the kingdom of the third king, who turns away from the page guarding the horses in the half-light, and advances with a vase in his outstretched hand. Through him the subject is invested with a grandeur that matches the magic of the setting.

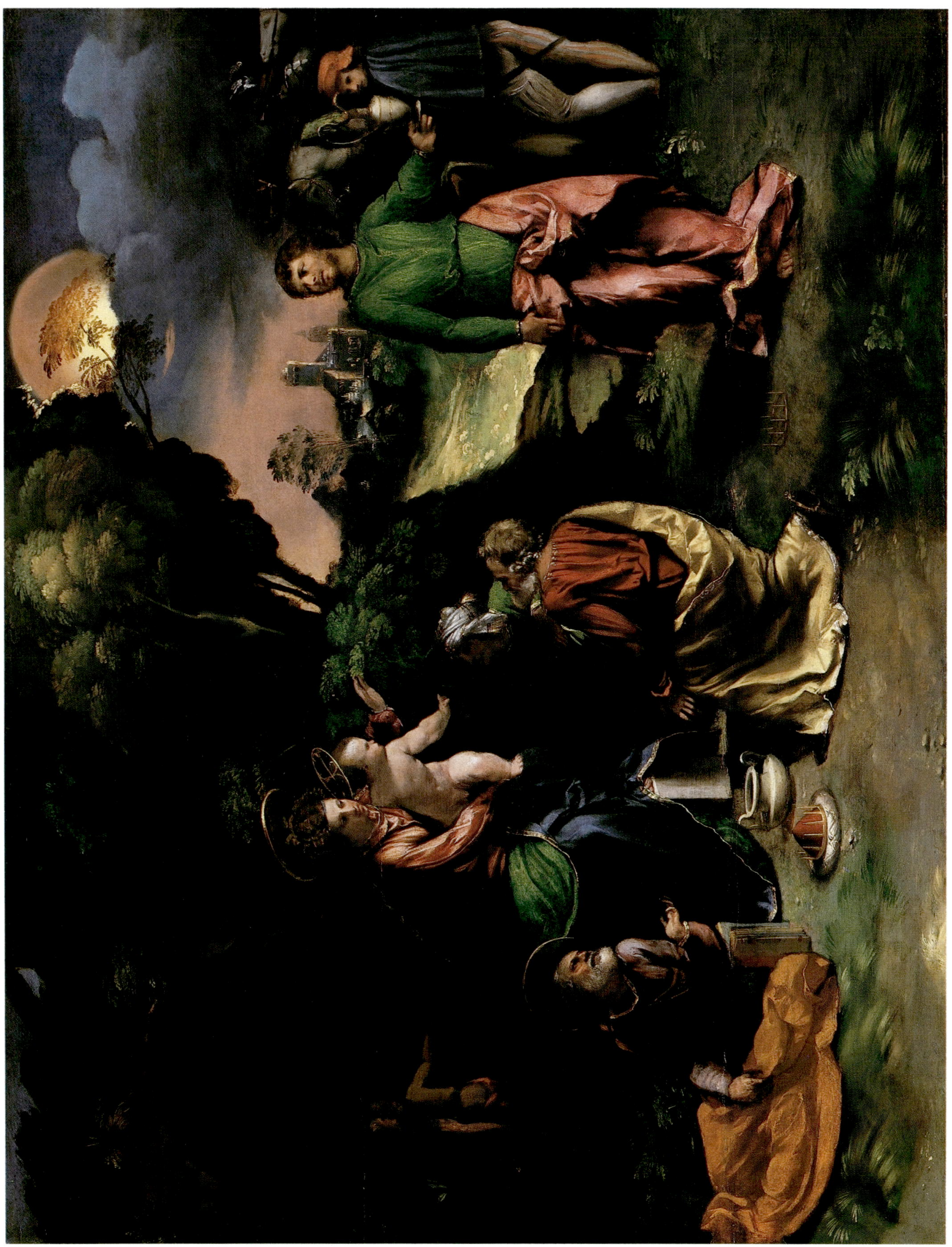

Jacopo Bassano, active about 1535; died 1592

The Way to Calvary (No. 6490)

Canvas, 145 × 133 cm.
Purchased 1984

The work of Jacopo Bassano, like that of Lotto (Plates 35, 36) at an earlier date, shows a great artist conjuring from the Venetian tradition new possibilities of design and expressive intensity. The son of a local painter of the town of Bassano in the hills to the north of Venice, Jacopo dal Ponte continued his father's practice after a period of training in Venice, and fathered four sons who in turn assisted with the many commissions that the studio continued to receive. The Bassano workshop was famous for popularizing night scenes, and for subjects which required the portrayal of animals – a talent that inevitably attracted English collectors to their works. Some of the greatest paintings of Jacopo Bassano are loosely organized depictions of such subjects as the Adoration of the Shepherds, but he was also alive, through the medium of prints, to the elegance of painting elsewhere in Italy, particularly in Parma, and to the achievements of German art.

Much of this is apparent in his *Way to Calvary*, an early masterpiece of about 1540, and one of a group of paintings which show a sudden widening of the painter's horizons before the more specialized work of his later years. The subject itself was frequently represented in sixteenth-century altarpieces (including one by Raphael), though rarely with such poignancy. Bassano adopts a densely crowded design of the kind more familiar from central Italian painting (Plate 23), and in this way conveys the turbulence of the melancholy procession, momentarily halted to reveal a scene of humble charity. With the exception of the soldier seen from the back in the centre, the figures are not classical or sculptural in effect, but thickly painted and coloured forms, carried out on canvas, and touched with the pathos of northern art and something of its ornamental expressiveness, which is particularly evident in the drapery of Christ.

A moment of calm is pictured in the foreground as Christ stumbles under the weight of the Cross and S. Veronica, kneeling, stretches out to him her veil, on which his features were to remain miraculously imprinted. The white of the veil is contrasted with the saturated pink of Christ's robe and with the sleeve of S. Veronica emerging from her brick-coloured dress in shades of lilac and green, as though to complement the spiritual significance of the veil. Sealing the composition in the corner is her pleated cream-coloured skirt which balances the severed tree on the left, marking the opposite corner and emphasizing the fact of the Cross. The weeping Virgin is shown to the right counterpoised to the figure of Christ, with S. John behind her, contrasted with the central soldier, and the other two Maries at her side, stretching forward with downcast eyes. Almost hidden in the upper corner but apparently observed by the soldier are two mounted figures, one with a crescent in his hat, a reminder of the persecutions that Christendom continued to face from the East in the lifetime of the painter.

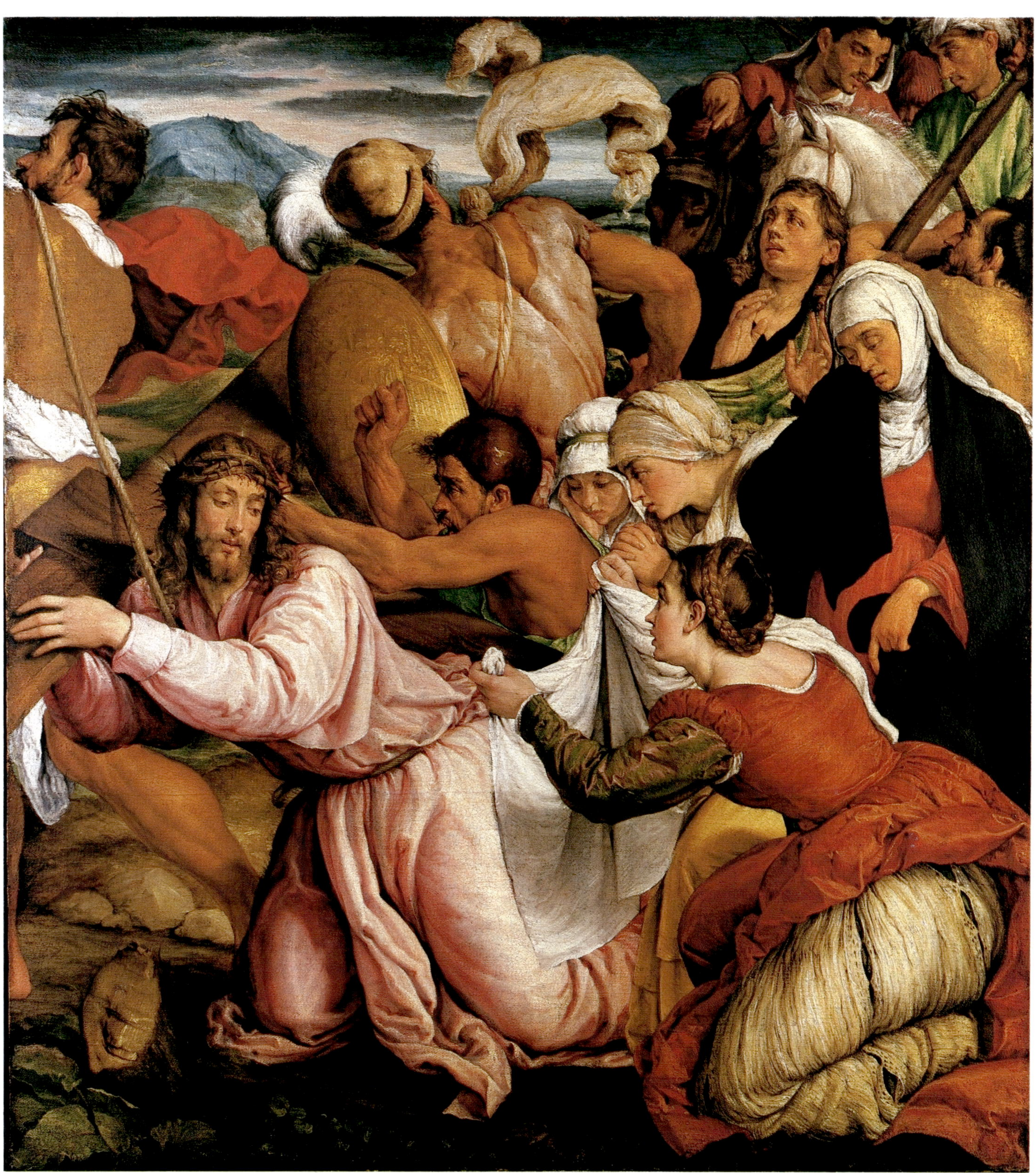

Titian, active before 1511; died 1576

The Vendramin Family (No. 4452)

Canvas, 205.7 × 301 cm.
Purchased 1929

Having witnessed the emergence of the High Renaissance in Venice, the late works of Giovanni Bellini and the career of Giorgione, Titian lived on until the 1570s, his style continually evolving until the very end of his long life, and constituting an antidote to the art of Michelangelo, whose work Titian experienced at first hand on a visit to Rome in 1545. His portrait of the Vendramin family was probably painted in the earlier 1540s, a painting that has been famous as an item of British heritage since the early seventeenth century, when it was owned by Van Dyck.

Freely painted on a large, coarsely woven canvas, it shows members of the Vendramin family at worship before an altar. A figure group of the Virgin and Child was normally the focus for votive paintings of this type, but here the painter has substituted an altar supporting a reliquary and candlesticks. The reliquary was one that belonged to the Vendramin family; it contained a fragment of the True Cross, and still exists in Venice at the Scuola of S. Giovanni Evangelista. It had been presented to a member of the Vendramin family in the fourteenth century, and had later been miraculously rescued by a Vendramin from submersion in the waters of the Grand Canal.

The noble figures of the older Vendramins, dressed in senators' robes, look upwards to the Cross, and they themselves are raised on high for their posterity to admire. Andrea Vendramin stretches out his arm as though inviting participation from the spectator, and a pathway to the altar is left clear in the centre of the painting. Titian compressed the composition on the left, and an earlier attempt at painting the head of the youngest bearded figure can be seen at the edge, no longer fully concealed by the blue of the sky.

Solemnity is the keynote of the scene for the older members of the family, but Titian's sympathy for the peculiarities of human and animal behaviour is present throughout. Gabriel Vendramin uses the altar to support his kneeling frame. Though placed higher in the painting than Andrea Vendramin, his junior in years and the father of the seven boys, he ranks only second in the composition. The elder boys grouped together on the left apprehend the gravity of the occasion, while the youngest three, placed out of sight of the reliquary to the right, behave with greater spontaneity. One dressed in green with scarlet tights, balancing like the scarf of Ariadne (Plate 15) the warm tones on the opposite side of the painting, perches with his pet dog on the step below the altar and, watched by the dog, his brothers tumble after him to the altar.

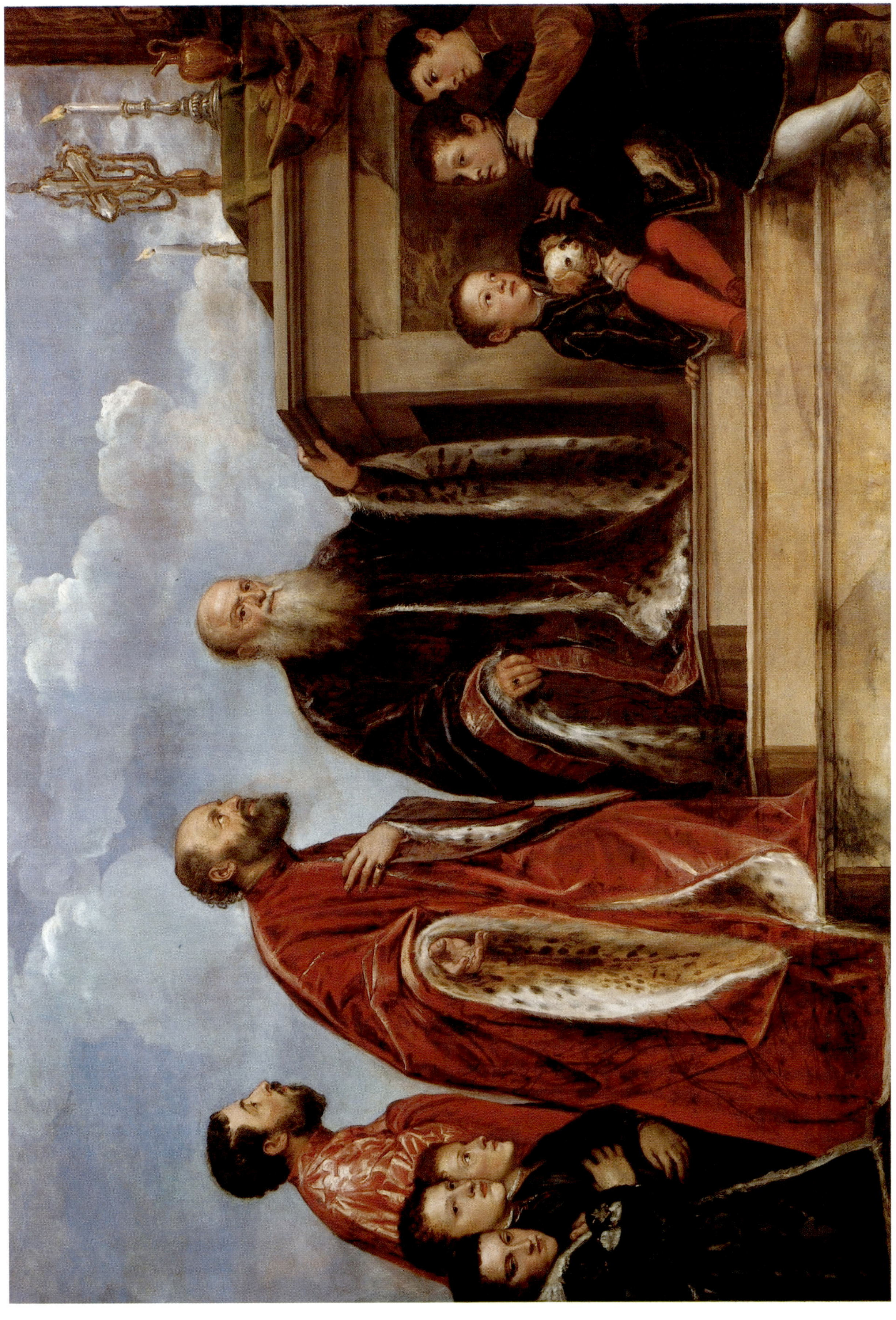

Titian, active before 1511; died 1576

The Death of Actaeon   (No. 6420)

Canvas, 178.4 × 198.1 cm.
Purchased, following a public appeal, 1972

Most famous of the later paintings of Titian are the series of large mythological scenes (*poesie*) painted for King Philip II of Spain in the 1550s and 1560s. Their subjects, mainly erotic in theme, were drawn from the *Metamorphoses* of Ovid, and several illustrate episodes of the story of Diana. A pair of paintings, now in the Sutherland collection (on loan to the National Gallery of Scotland), which were sent to the King probably in 1559, show Diana and her nymphs bathing, one with the discovery of the pregnancy of the nymph Callisto, and the other with Diana and Actaeon. Actaeon, in this most beautiful of the *poesie*, enters the painting on the left, accompanied by his hunting dogs, and discovers the naked figure of Diana surrounded by her attendants.

The Death of Actaeon illustrates the sequel. Actaeon is transformed into a stag by Diana, pursued and savaged to death by his own dogs. Here Actaeon appears on the right, partly transformed, with Diana pursuing him in the left foreground. At first Titian seems to have shown the goddess, who was not present in Ovid at the kill, brandishing her bow; he later altered this to convey the idea of Diana shooting at Actaeon, integrating the goddess more fully into the action, but hesitating to include the essential, if too specific, details of arrow and bow-string.

The painting was probably one on which the painter laboured for a long period. It may have been started in the later 1550s, and advanced in the following decade. Late in the 1560s the theme was one mentioned in a list of subjects painted by Titian sent to the Emperor Maximilian II, which brought the revealing reply from the Emperor that the painter was now too old to paint well. So personal had Titian's style become that his latest works, like those of Michelangelo, were intelligible to few of his contemporaries.

Subjects of pathos and melancholy accompanied the changed styles of both artists, and a remote story like the death of Actaeon assumes a disturbingly personal intensity. All the components in the painting, like the action of the goddess herself, are suggested but not supplied in any detail. The landscape is autumnal in its hue, merging with the colours of the dogs, their collars denoting Actaeon's ownership, as they pursue their master to his death. He falls backwards, and his fall is echoed in the landscape by the foremost tree in the glade behind. The running figure of Diana in sombre pink is amplified by the clouds and the shimmering water, which lend to the painting its overshadowing sense of universal tragedy.

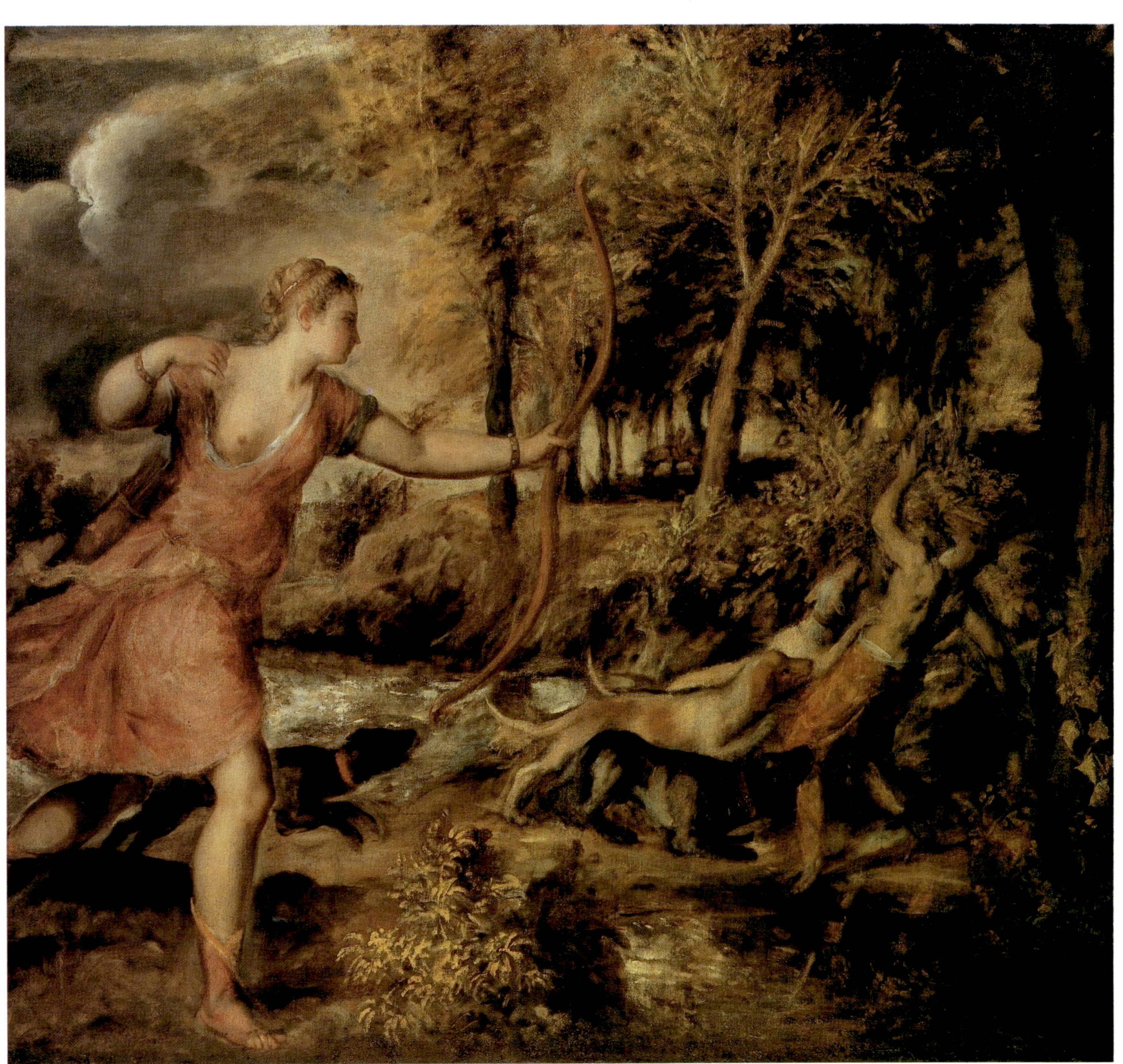

Titian, active before 1511; died 1576

Madonna and Child (No. 3948)

Canvas, 75.6 × 63.2 cm.
Mond Bequest 1924

On a smaller scale than *The Death of Actaeon*, the latest and most personal style of Titian is represented in the National Gallery by the only half-length Virgin and Child by the artist in the collection. It was probably painted during the course of his very last years – 'during the course' because it was Titian's habit at this date, not specifically for larger and more troublesome compositions, to retain his paintings in his studio and work on them over long periods, and thus they grew to maturity by an almost human process of growth and mutation.

The small Venetian Madonna composition, which had been brought to early perfection in the work of Bellini, was by no means common in sixteenth-century Venice. Titian's composition is thus something of a rarity, and unusual in theme in showing the Virgin suckling the Child (the 'Virgo lactans'), a subject that had long since lost its general popularity. A composition based on the shape of a pyramid links together the painted forms of the mother and child, their arms crossing in the centre and their legs symmetrically reversed.

The young face of the Virgin looks down at the Child, but the eyes of both are hidden from the spectator, showing that more than mere portraiture is intended. Subject and style are closely related since the function of the brushwork is to suggest rather than to define. The colours are dispersed and the forms softened to such an extent that they become coherent only from a distance. The broad body of the Madonna is clad not in rose and blue, but in a grey dress softened by warm brown shadows which blend with the flesh tones, with the red-fringed shawl, and in turn with the softly glowing fabric of the curtain to the right.

Methods of formal integration for compositions showing the Virgin and Child had been fundamental to the development of painting in the early sixteenth century, and the experiments of Leonardo (Plate 2) and Raphael cannot have remained entirely unknown to Titian. His own answer to the difficulties that such a group imposed upon the painter is of deceptive simplicity. The handling and colouring of the paint at this late moment in his career give both weight and natural softness to the figures, and serve to unify the painting, even as the figures themselves so intimately embrace.

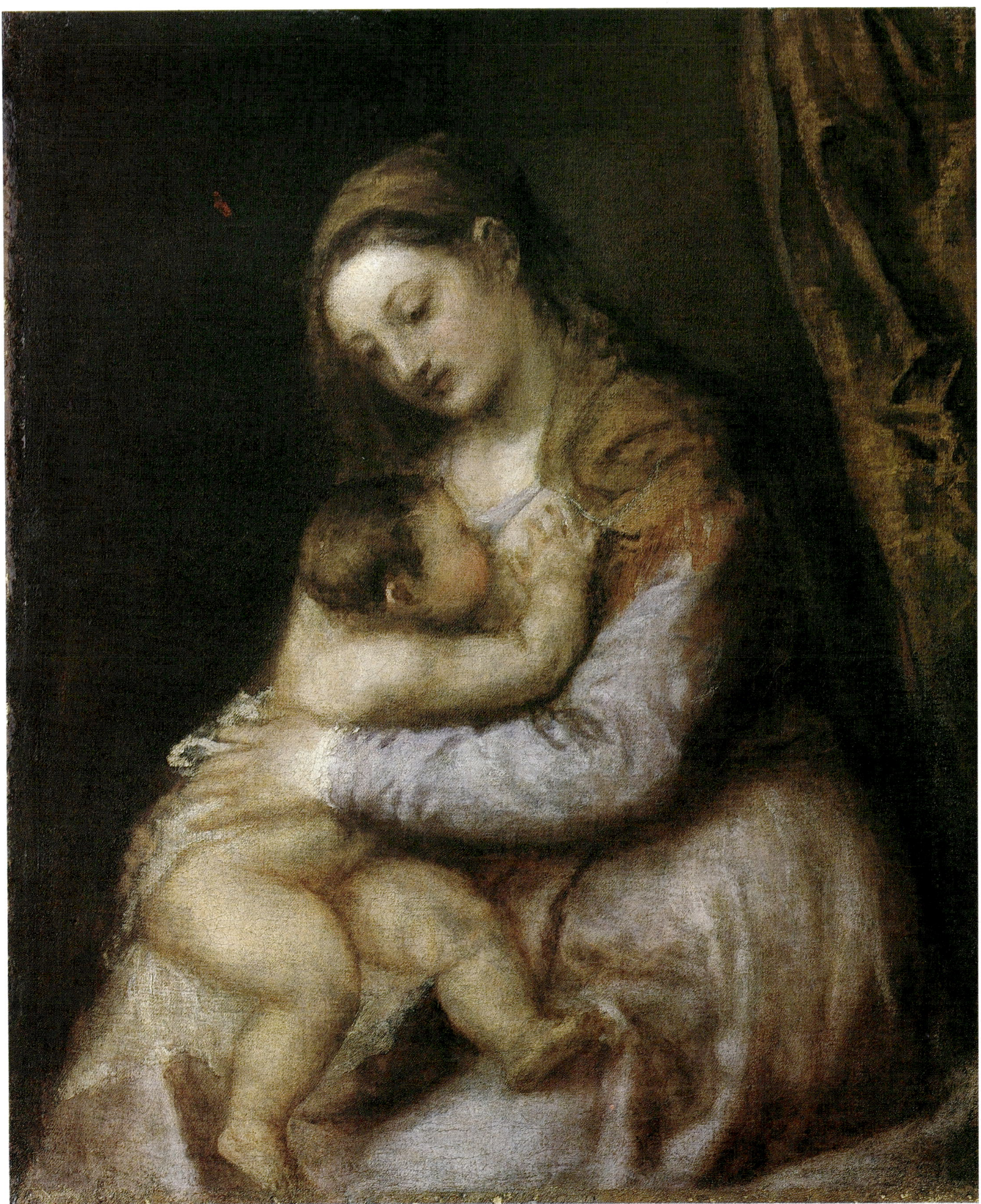

PLATE 42

Jacopo Tintoretto, 1518–1594

S. George and the Dragon (No. 16)

Canvas, 157.5 × 100.3 cm.
Holwell Carr Bequest 1831

Titian was more fortunate than Michelangelo in his direct followers, and in the hands of Tintoretto and Veronese the standard of Venetian art remained outstanding until the very last years of the sixteenth century, when Rome again established itself as the artistic capital of Italy. Jacopo Robusti, who received the name Tintoretto from his father's profession of dyer (*tintore*) was a Venetian by birth and active throughout his life in his native town, where his prolific genius is to be seen at its most inventive in the decorations carried out over many years in the Scuola of San Rocco.

To unite the colouring of Titian and the drawing of Michelangelo was considered the aim and the achievement of Tintoretto, and both artists were of fundamental importance to his work, but what he discovered in Michelangelo was a repertoire of images suited to his own leaning towards the expression of energy and irrational force, images which he re-created in a technique rich in colouring but not otherwise closely related to the handling of Titian. In preparation for many of his works he is known to have experimented like a stage designer with grouping and lighting small-scale lay figures for his compositions.

S. George and the Dragon, probably an early work of the 1550s or 1560s and originally an altarpiece for a private chapel, shows how the style Tintoretto evolved could transform a scene of such potential drama. Excitement is communicated by the very handling of the paint, in the agitated draperies and the tormented, almost Germanic, landscape that forms the setting of the scene. Tintoretto has departed in many ways from the traditional manner of representing this familiar subject, not least in assigning the major role in the action not to the saint but to the princess he is rescuing from the dragon. An intensely expressive figure, dressed in blue and rose, the colours of the Virgin, she seems to have dropped to her knees in the agitation of flight, and in this key of fear and apprehension the composition unfolds.

It moves along the seashore, beginning with the trunk of a lone tree that counters the swaying posture of the maiden. In the centre of the canvas is the splendid armoured figure of the saint on his plunging white horse driving the dragon into the sea, and lastly the brilliant vision in the sky of Christ blessing the saint. This unexpected and dramatic innovation and the emphasis given to the maiden presumably reflect shades of new meaning which the patron wished to see incorporated in the painting, and which the artist interpreted with unexampled vigour and ingenuity.

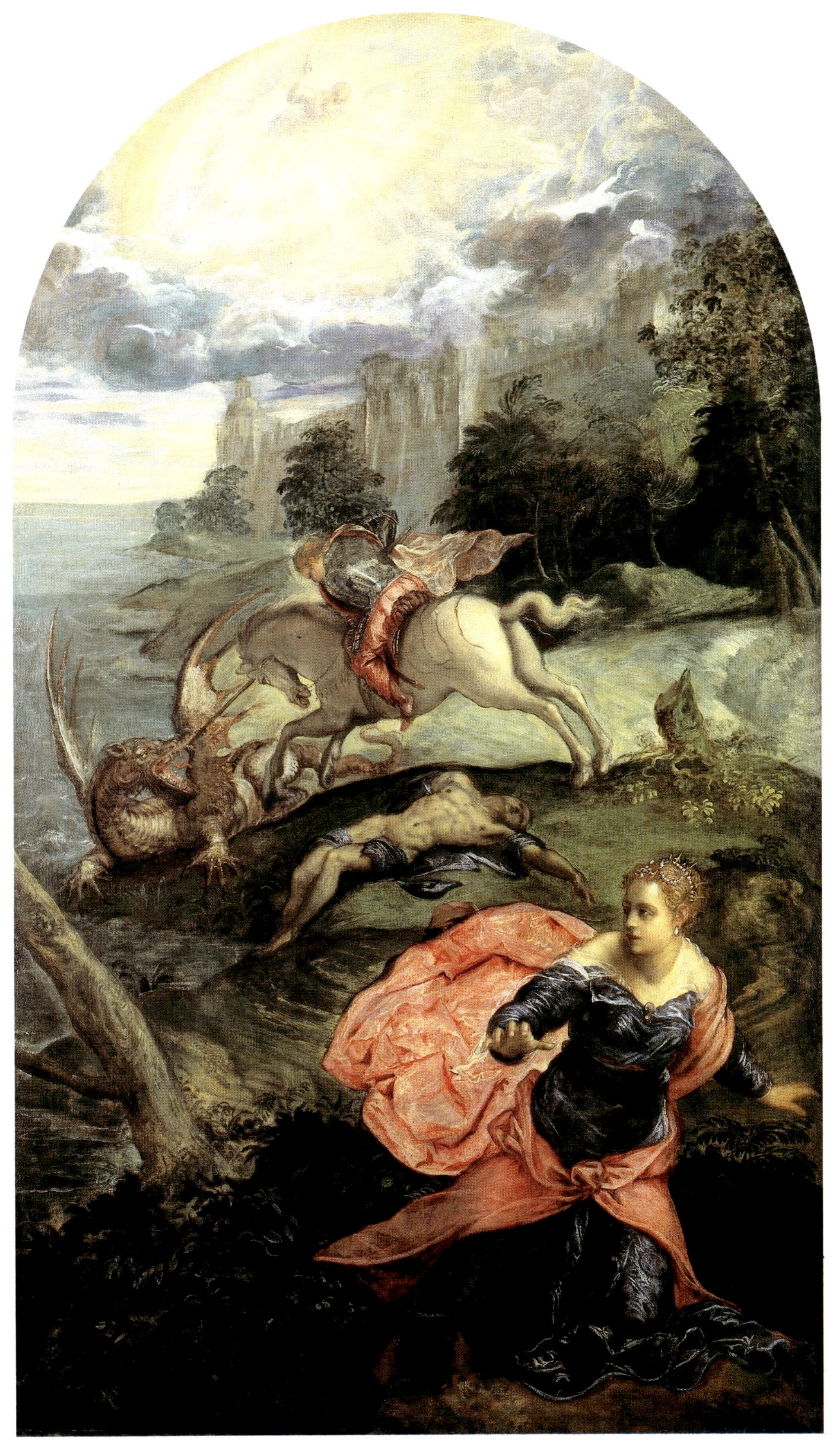

Jacopo Tintoretto, 1518–1594

The Origin of the Milky Way (No. 1313)

Canvas, 148 × 165.1 cm.
Purchased 1890

Tintoretto swiftly acquired mastery in painting the human body in every variety of pose, allowing him at the last to formulate compelling compositions for traditional subjects and others as yet untried. His works became, like the frescoes of Correggio, a source of inspiration for the visionary art of the Counter-Reformation in the following century, though the more reflective emanations of Renaissance art, which Correggio shared with Titian in transmitting to posterity, lose importance in his work, and there is present, especially in many of his religious paintings, a turbulence scarcely justified by the requirements of the story. The gods of antiquity, on the other hand, make their appearance in his canvases with a verve and brilliance that enhance with a new sense of exhilaration the miraculous events of their lives.

The Origin of the Milky Way is probably a work of the 1570s, and probably also one of a series of four paintings carried out for the Emperor Rudolf II. It illustrates the obscure story of Jupiter conferring immortality on his half-human son, Hercules, by holding him to the breast of the sleeping goddess Juno. Milk continued to flow from her breasts when the child was thrown off, one stream spilling upwards, where it formed the stars of the Milky Way, and one falling to earth creating the lily. Originally the painting showed at the base a figure reclining on the earth with lilies at her feet, but the canvas was cut at an early date and this part of the painting is missing.

Tintoretto has pictured the scene at its most dramatic juncture, as Juno suddenly awakens and rises from her air-borne bed. She twists her body from the mouth of Hercules, who is held up by Jupiter, a wingless figure with wind-blown hair and a billowing red and blue cloak, suspended dramatically above her in the sky. The gesturing arms of Juno indicate alarm and protest, but they also emphasize the creation of the stars and the more distant propagation of the lily.

The eagle bearing thunderbolts that is symbolic of Jupiter turns in profile towards the two peacocks on the right, birds that are an attribute of Juno. Four winged *amorini*, holding objects symbolic of love and of its snares – a bow and arrows, chains and a net – are shown in foreshortened poses and add still further to the pictorial and psychological complexity of the scene.

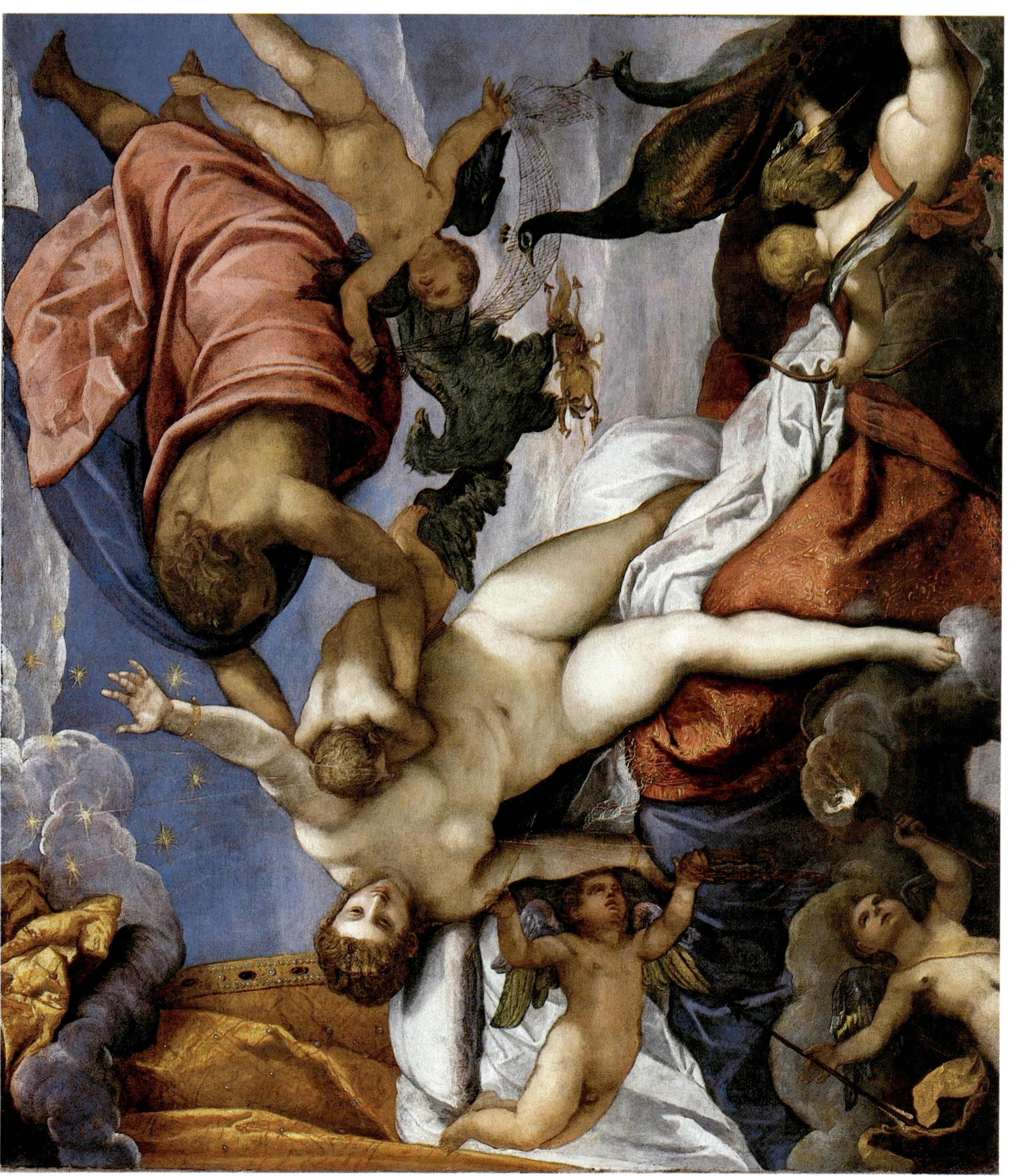

Jacopo Tintoretto, 1518–1594

Portrait of Vincenzo Morosini (No. 4004)

Canvas, 84.5 × 51.5 cm.
Presented by the National Art-Collections Fund 1924

Like Titian, Tintoretto produced many portraits throughout the course of his long career, though his style was not naturally well adapted to portraiture and the results of his efforts, nearly all head-and-shoulders or half-lengths of male sitters, are uneven in quality, many betraying an evident impatience with the restrictions of the discipline. The portrait of Vincenzo Morosini, a late work probably of about 1585, is amongst the more memorable of Tintoretto's portraits.

The sitter (1511–1588) was then in his mid-seventies, a member of a noble Venetian family, who had served as Prefect of Bergamo in 1555. More recently he had become a Procurator of S. Mark's, and in 1584 President of the University of Padua. A similar representation of him by Tintoretto appears in the *Resurrection*, painted for the Morosini family chapel in S. Giorgio Maggiore.

The portrait is unusual in its narrow format and, though its shape accords not unsympathetically with the long cast of the sitter's features, it was probably originally of a wider and more conven-tional size and later cut down at the sides and base. The sitter's cuff appears at the bottom of the canvas, though the hand is not now visible, and the presentation of the upper part of the body, and not least the breadth of the handling, seems constrained by the present limitations of the canvas.

The senator's robe is indicated by no more than a dozen or so strokes of rose-coloured paint on a crimson ground, and the patterned embroideries of the golden stole (the *stola d'oro*, the badge of Venetian knighthood), which falls in a straight line from the sitter's shoulder, by no more than a few lines and stippling of yellow and white. Similarly the narrow glimpse of landscape on the right, presumably more extensive originally, is shaped from an almost abstract pattern of green and white shading into blue. In contrast with the brilliant impatience of these details is the more carefully studied head, a face of shrewdness and penetration which the painter no less skilfully represents, look-ing with a certain caution from the canvas.

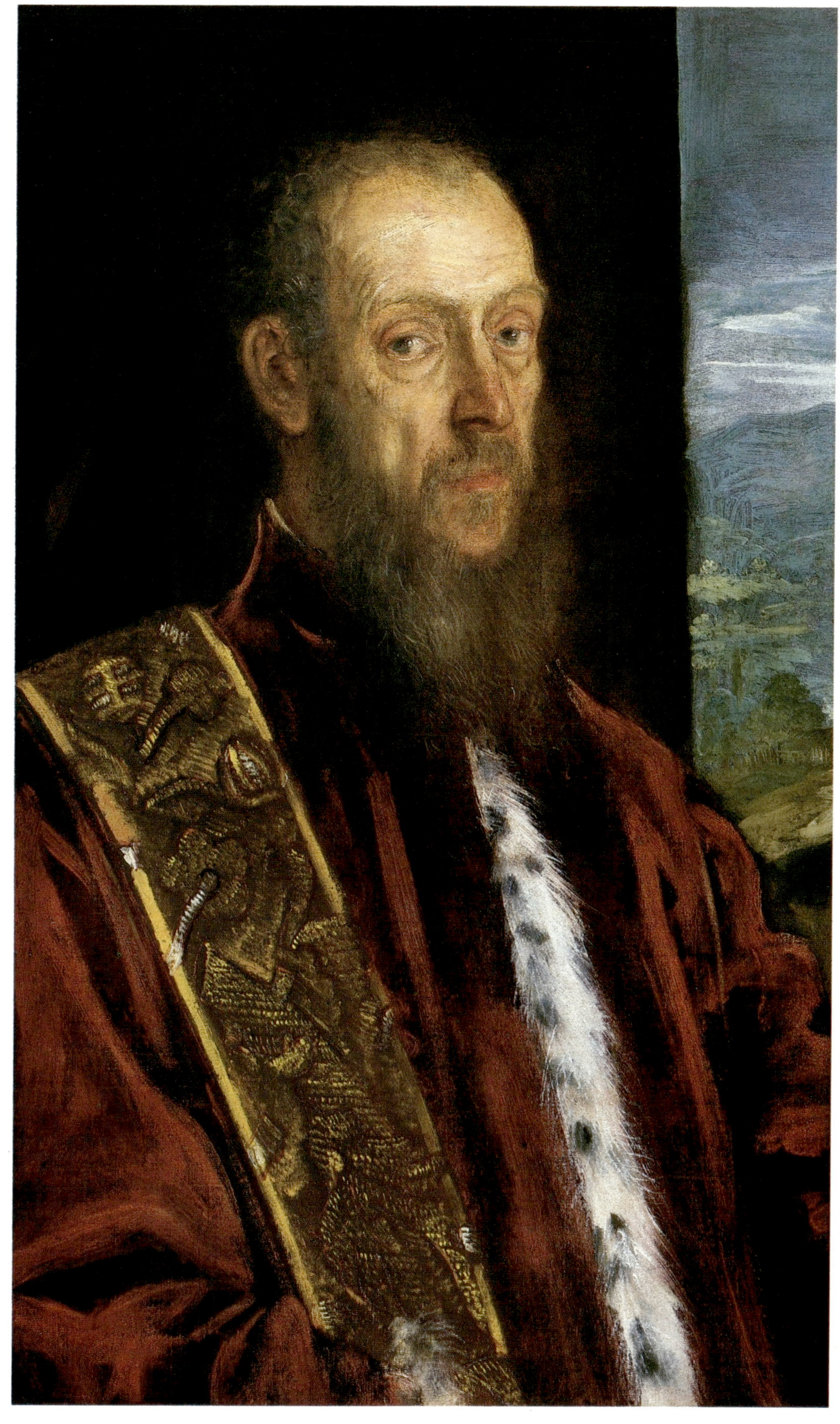

Paolo Veronese, 1528(?)–1588

The Consecration of S. Nicholas (No. 26)

Canvas, *c.* 283 × 171 cm.
Presented by the Governors of the British Institution 1826

Tintoretto's main rival in Venice in the later six-teenth century was his slightly younger contem-porary, Veronese, and patrons unresponsive to Tintoretto's energetic work could find an alterna-tive in the sumptuous and elegant art of Veronese. Facility and ease are so greatly in evidence in Veronese's paintings that his aims to this extent coincide with those of Michelangelo's followers, but with Titian as a starting-point the effects of splen-dour in his paintings give the appearance of de-riving largely from the world of visible reality. His work was fundamental to the development of painting in eighteenth-century Venice and the art of Tiepolo.

Paolo Caliari was born in Verona, whence the name 'Veronese' derives, and he came as a young man in his twenties to Venice, living there for the remainder of his years. His output, great in number and often in scale, also covered a wide range of subject-matter. Like Tintoretto, he established a personal style at an early date and remained faithful to its principles thereafter, so that few of his paintings can be dated with precision.

The Consecration of S. Nicholas is known to be a comparatively early work, one of two surviving altarpieces of a group of three painted in 1561–62 for the church of S. Benedetto Po near Mantua. It tells the story of S. Nicholas, when a young priest, being chosen by divine intervention to succeed to the Archbishopric of Myra in Lycia. S. Nicholas is the kneeling figure dressed in brilliant green at the foot of the steps, and the focus of the composi-tion lies in the Archbishop's hand, the glove marked with the sign of Christ's stigmata, which is stretched emphatically over his head. He is encircled, almost hidden, by the venerable priests at his side whose white robes set off the colours of the main actors in the manner pioneered by Titian.

As in Titian's *The Vendramin Family* (Plate 39), the boy on the steps to the right, helping to support the archbishop's cross, wears brilliant scarlet stockings, together with the green, gold and white that appear on the left of the composition. The archbishop himself is distinguished by an intense blue vestment, probably of the precious pigment of ultramarine, suggesting the opulence of the Church – and its authority, too, is adumbrated in the painting, by the inclusion of just the corner of the magnificent building where the Archbishop stands. On the left two spectators are introduced wearing turbans, which indicate the eastern setting of the miracle, and crossing the composition from right to left at the summit – as though forcibly diverted from the old to the new archbishop – a golden-haired angel descends bearing heaven-sent accoutrements, notably the crozier and mitre, for the investiture of the saint.

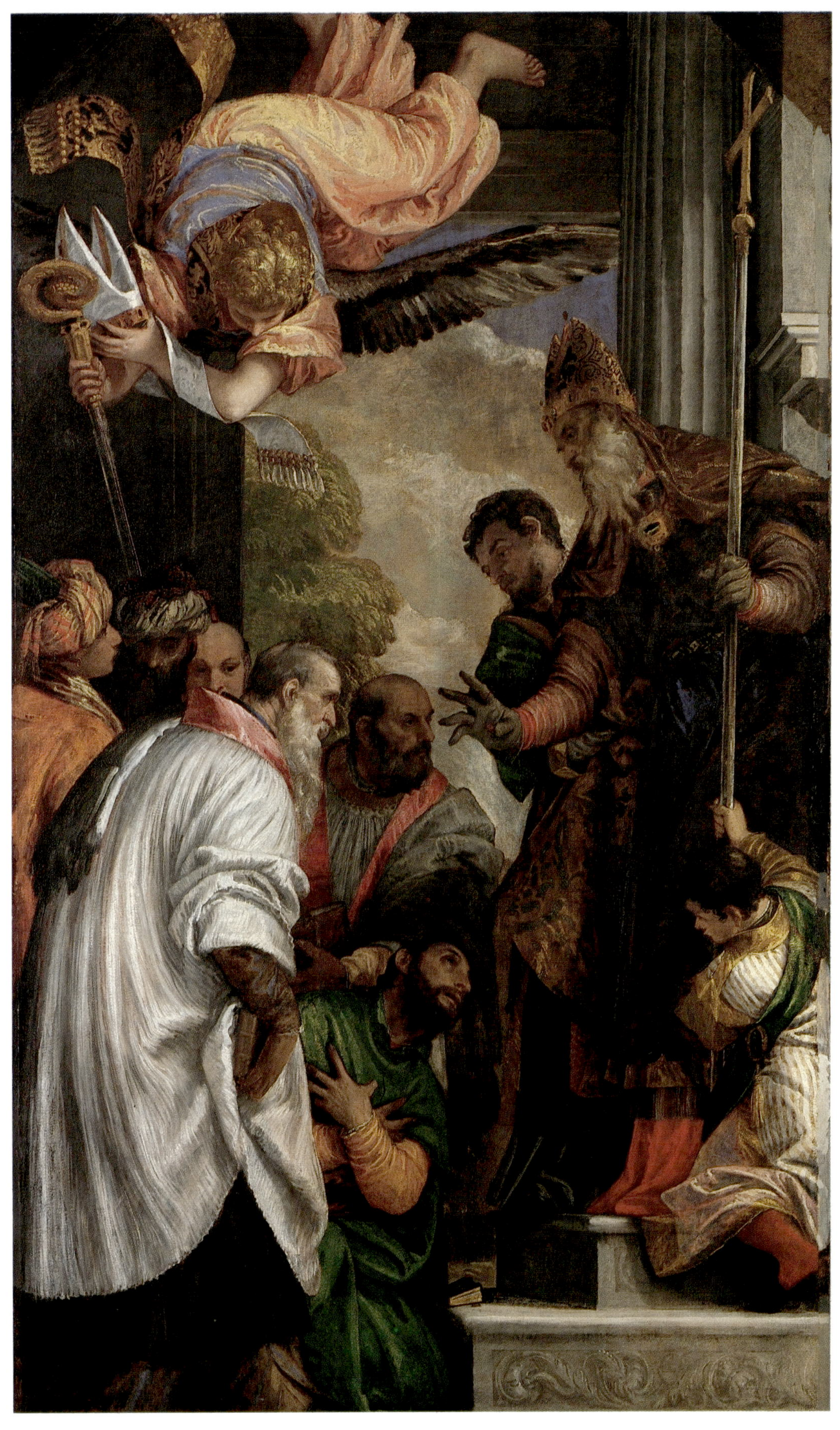

PLATE 46

Paolo Veronese, 1528(?)–1588

The Family of Darius before Alexander (No. 294)

Canvas, 236 × 475 cm.
Purchased 1857

Historical pageantry provided the subjects perhaps best suited to Veronese's art, and the most famous of his paintings in the National Gallery is his large *Family of Darius before Alexander*. The later religious paintings of the artist became so weighted with secular detail that he was examined in 1573 by a tribunal of the Inquisition about a '*Last Supper*', later entitled '*Feast in the House of Simon*' (Accademia, Venice). The glimpses of Veronese's personality afforded by the proceedings of the trial show a practical mind of disarming simplicity and give little hint of his acute pictorial intelligence.

His painting of Alexander was acquired in Venice from a descendant of the Pisani family, and was probably commissioned for their palace in Venice in the 1570s. The theme is one illustrating generosity in victory, a subject of relevance to the education of princes and nobles, and one that presumably held special significance for the patron. East and west are confronted in the painting, like Venice and its oriental empire, and all is subservient to the dominant male hero, who alone wears red, intensified with pink. This must be Alexander, and the painting takes its subject from his magnanimous behaviour to the family – the mother, wife and two daughters – of the defeated Persian king, Darius. Agitated and tearful, they had at first mistaken Hephaestion, presumably the foreground figure in gold and yellow, for Alexander himself. In the picture he is calming their fears, and renouncing his claims as conqueror over the distraught family of his defeated enemy.

The counterpoint of gesture, pose and colour adopted for the four main actors, the mother and wife of Darius, and Alexander and his friend, is supported by the massing of the composition. The victorious Macedonian troops intrude in a dense group into the palace of Darius, where the centre of the terrace is occupied by the Persian queen. Behind are her grandchildren, and a handful of exotic retainers and pets, with a monkey dangling the chain of his own captivity. A hunting dog restrained by a soldier on the right is compared with lap-dogs comforted by a dwarf on the left.

The centre of the court is occupied by a giant pedestal with niches and statues and what may be an oriental obelisk at its summit. Recession into the background is achieved by the dilution of the colours and the increasing freedom of the brushwork. The palace resembles a Palladian mansion on a giant scale, just as many of the figures wear contemporary dress, and in this way the story of Alexander's generosity, matchlessly conveyed by the painter, also possesses an intelligible contemporary relevance.

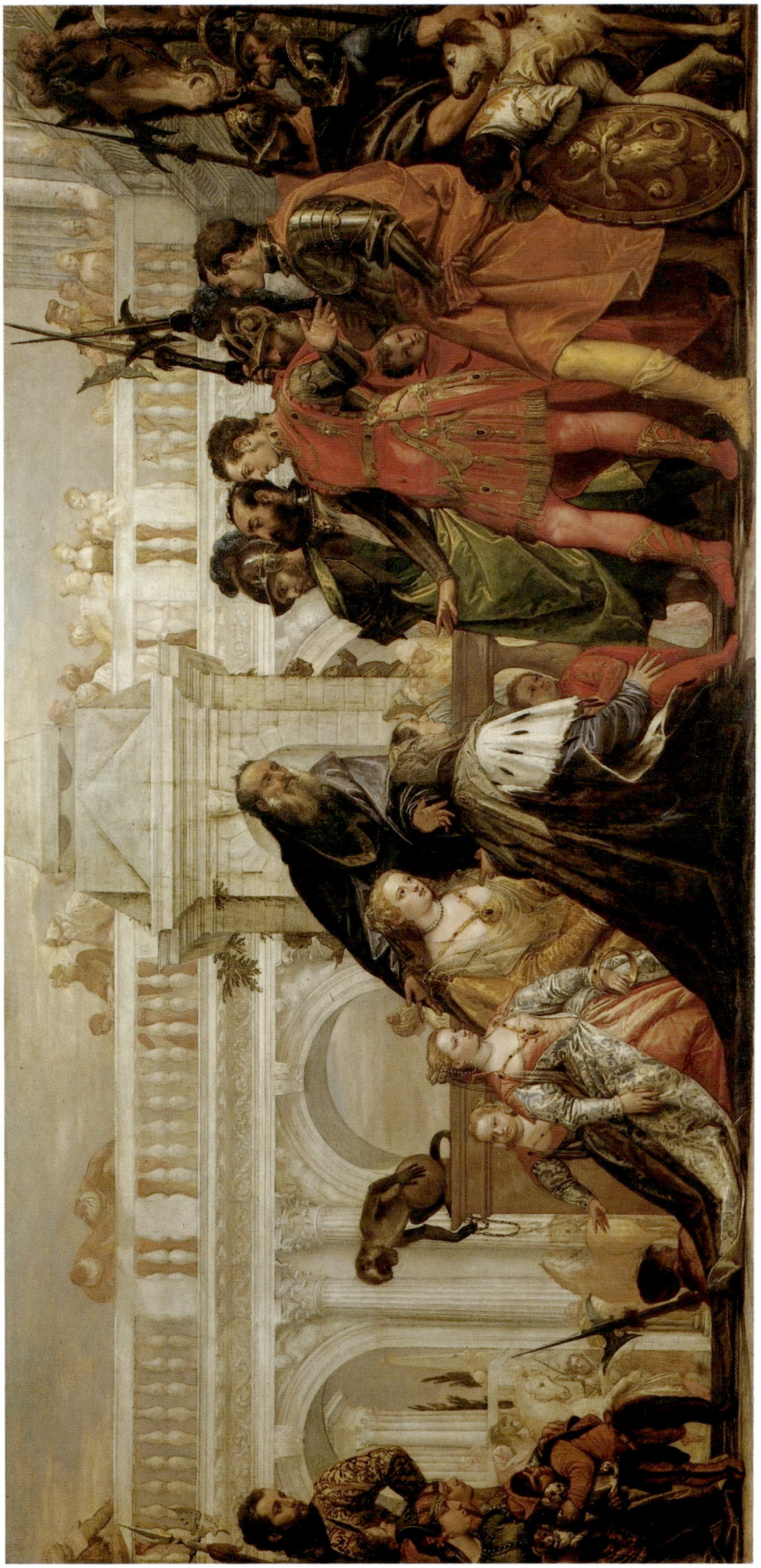

Paolo Veronese, 1528(?)–1588

Allegory of Love, I ('Unfaithfulness') (No. 1318)

Inscribed on the letter
Canvas, 190 × 190 cm.
Purchased 1890

This *Allegory of Love* is one of a set of four paintings by Veronese in the National Gallery, probably compositions of the 1570s designed for the decoration of a ceiling. Nothing is known of the early history of the paintings and the exact nature of the subject-matter remains undiscovered. In the present painting a naked woman sits with two male companions in a landscape. The man on her right holds up her arm and gazes at her body, while the one to her left, dressed more richly, seems indifferent to her. She turns towards him and passes a letter into his hand. The composition appears to be an illustration of unfaithfulness, and this was the title given to the painting in the eighteenth century.

The form established by Titian for ceiling paintings in Venice is followed here by Veronese, as in the many other such decorations he was called upon to execute. The figures are shown from below at a steep angle to the spectator, and such compositions were generally framed between wooden ceiling beams, themselves painted or richly carved and gilded. The directness and relative simplicity of the paintings in composition, and the freedom of the handling, with strongly marked contours and changes left largely visible, reflect the function for which they were painted, the distance from which they were to be surveyed and the shared part each played in the disposition of the ceiling.

Of the four allegories the present one is the most daring in composition, taking as its centrepiece the woman's back, which Veronese imbues with the voluptuous breadth that Titian had introduced into Venetian painting, and the expertise in foreshortening that was the speciality of Tintoretto. It establishes the erotic mood of the painting by its very discretion, the boy in the foreground apparently helping the woman to show herself to the abstracted man, while the winged Cupid on the left looks towards the woman and plays upon a portable keyboard. Characteristic of the painter's visual sensitivity is the treatment of the landscape, which mirrors the action of the humans. The green lining of the woman's drapery is reflected in the foliage of the trees, two of the same robust species overlapping on the right, and one stretching across the painting towards the paler tree on the left, which is more delicately branching and softer in its colouring.

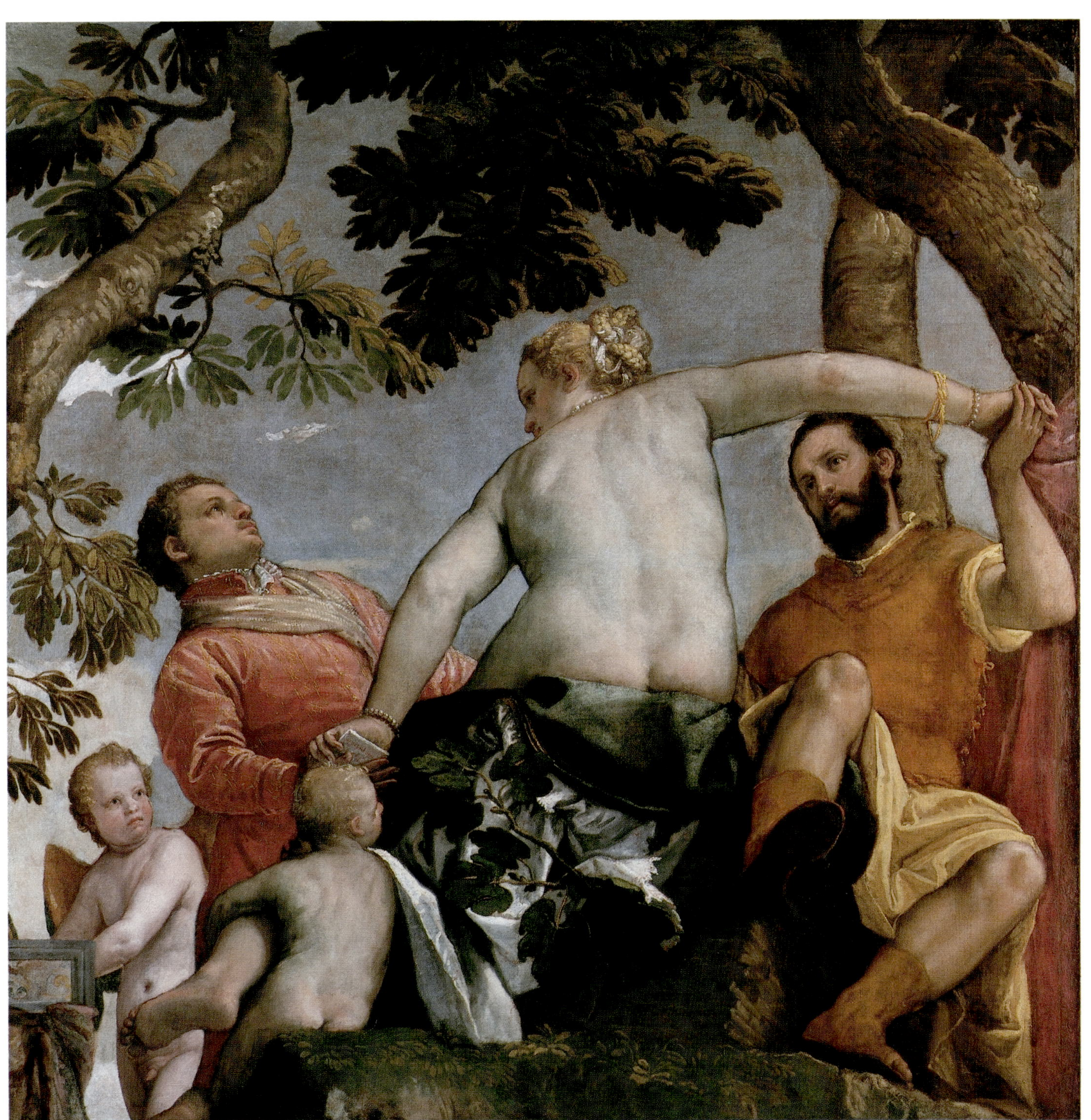

Paolo Veronese, 1528(?)–1588

Allegory of Love, IV ('Happy Union') (No. 1326)

Canvas, 187 × 187 cm.
Purchased 1891

Allegory of Love, IV, is probably the last in the sequence of Veronese's four allegories in the National Gallery, a scene of fulfilment and conjugal felicity that forms an evident contrast to the other three episodes illustrated by the painter. It is indeed likely that the series had a serious moral purpose, and may well have been commissioned to commemorate an important wedding.

The principal figure in the fourth allegory is not naked but dressed in a sumptuous gown of rose, patterned with gold. It forms a pyramid of colour in the centre of the canvas, establishing strong diagonal axes that would have been taken up in the other allegories, each of which is designed with pronounced crossing rhythms (Plate 47). The figure here wears a ring prominently displayed on her right hand, an elaborate brooch, and a necklace of pearls clasped around her neck as she stretches upwards to receive a crown of leaves held over her head. This is held out by a naked female figure sitting on a globe with a cornucopia at her side and a green marble column behind her, its Ionic capital projecting at the level of her head. The figure is most probably an incarnation of Venus in a chaste guise, as the veil and girdle would indicate, and hence her likely significance is conjugal love. The crown itself appears to be of myrtle, a plant sacred to Venus, while the globe would refer to the universality of her power and the cornucopia to the material blessings which should be the reward of virtue.

To the right, and dressed in green and gold, which reflect the colours surrounding the visionary figure on the left, is the woman's partner, jointly holding with her an olive branch that denotes peace. The contours of the arms seen against the sky are painted with conspicuous freedom, imbued with the suggestion of movement in the air and giving emphasis to gestures whose import the spectator would have been obliged to apprehend from a distance. The final participants in the scene are the boy who holds a chain binding the woman, and the lively dog, denoting fidelity, which gazes with near-human anxiety towards the apparition that has materialized to reward the couple.

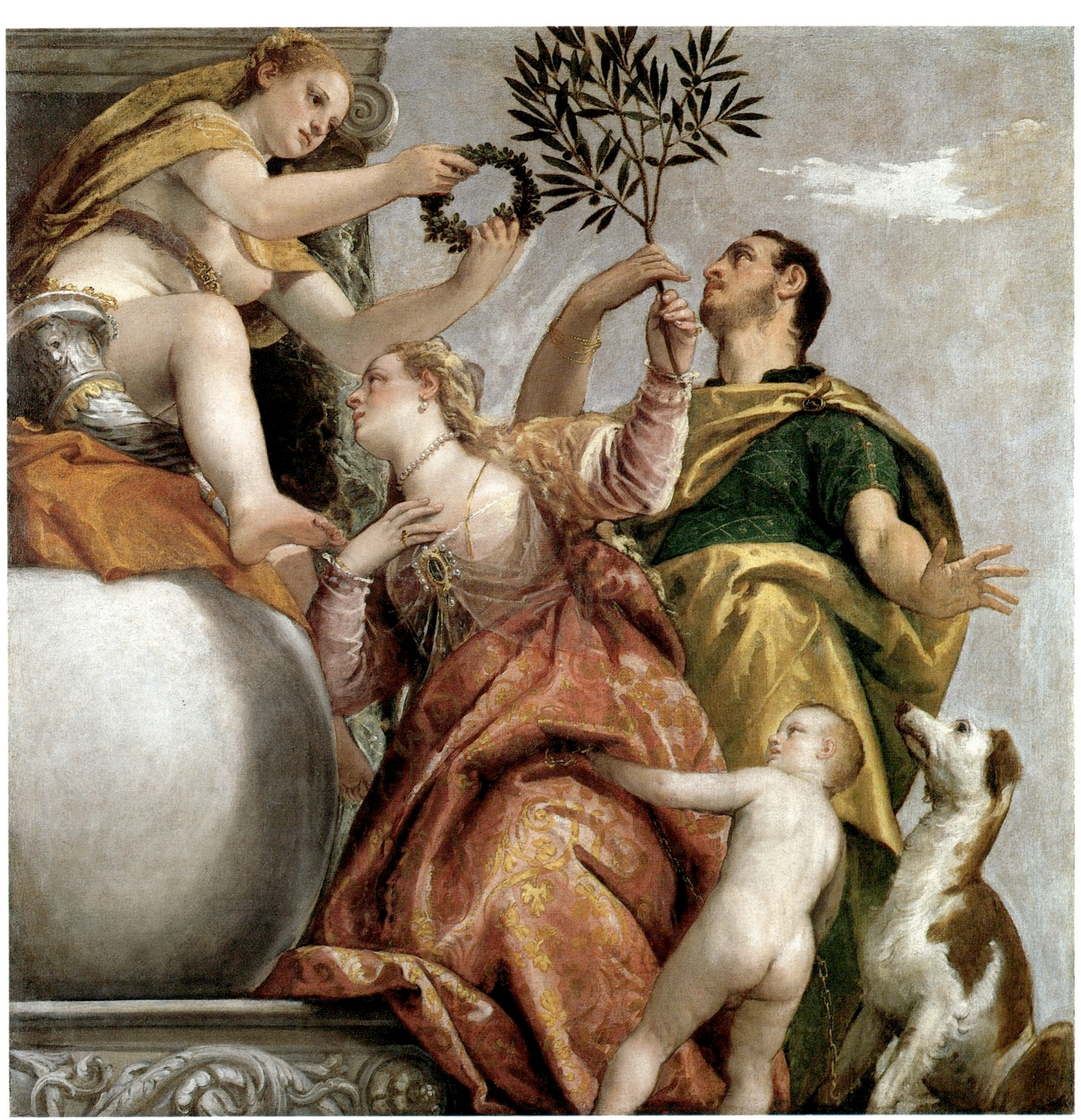

Giovan Battista Moroni, active 1546/7; died 1578

Portrait of a Gentleman (No. 1022)

Canvas, 202.2 × 106 cm.
Purchased 1876

Giovan Battista Moroni, the great exponent of the portrait in the later sixteenth century in Italy, was born near Albino, a small town in the foothills of the Alps to the north of Bergamo. His training took place in Brescia with Moretto (Plate 33), whose compositions for religious painting Moroni continued to use, where possible, throughout the course of his career. Following Moretto's death in 1554, his activity was centred in the Bergamo–Albino area, and here in his portraits he revealed a talent very different from Moretto's in the depiction of contemporaries from many walks of life.

His *Portrait of a Gentleman* is probably of the later 1550s, a painting traditionally entitled '*The Knight with a wounded Foot*' because of the brace which the sitter wears on his left leg. It was acquired from the same collection in Brescia as Moretto's portrait of 1526 (Plate 33) and may well represent one of the two sons of Moretto's sitter, Pietro or Faustino Avogadro. Like Moretto, Moroni shows his sitter at full length in an architectural setting, but the impression conveyed by the portrait is by no means idealized or lacking in psychological urgency, and in this it departs from the normal conventions of the earlier sixteenth century, emphasizing even the frailty of man, as in a modern portrait.

The man is shown from the side equipped with the clothes usually worn under a suit of armour, though the narrow silhouette seems scarcely capable of bearing the weight of armour strewn upon the floor or the extravagantly plumed helmet on which his arm rests. Except for the red badge over the plumes the colours are entirely muted, the feathers of the hat keyed in hue with the clothes of the sitter and the marbled panels of the architecture. The head turns from the direction of the helmet to face outwards, looking guardedly from the corners of the eyes. The architecture defines the outline of the pose, as adumbrated by Moretto, but here the building is partly ruined, more extensively stained, and penetrated with shrubs and ivy at the level of the head. Moroni had first introduced ruined architecture in a portrait of 1554 (Ambrosiana, Milan) for a sitter whose motto, prominently displayed in the painting, was 'Impavidum ferient ruinae', meaning roughly 'fearless amongst the ruins'. This is probably the sense in which ruins in his later portraits should be interpreted, although they also play their part in underlining the transience of human endeavour, the impression conveyed by the painter's approach to his sitters.

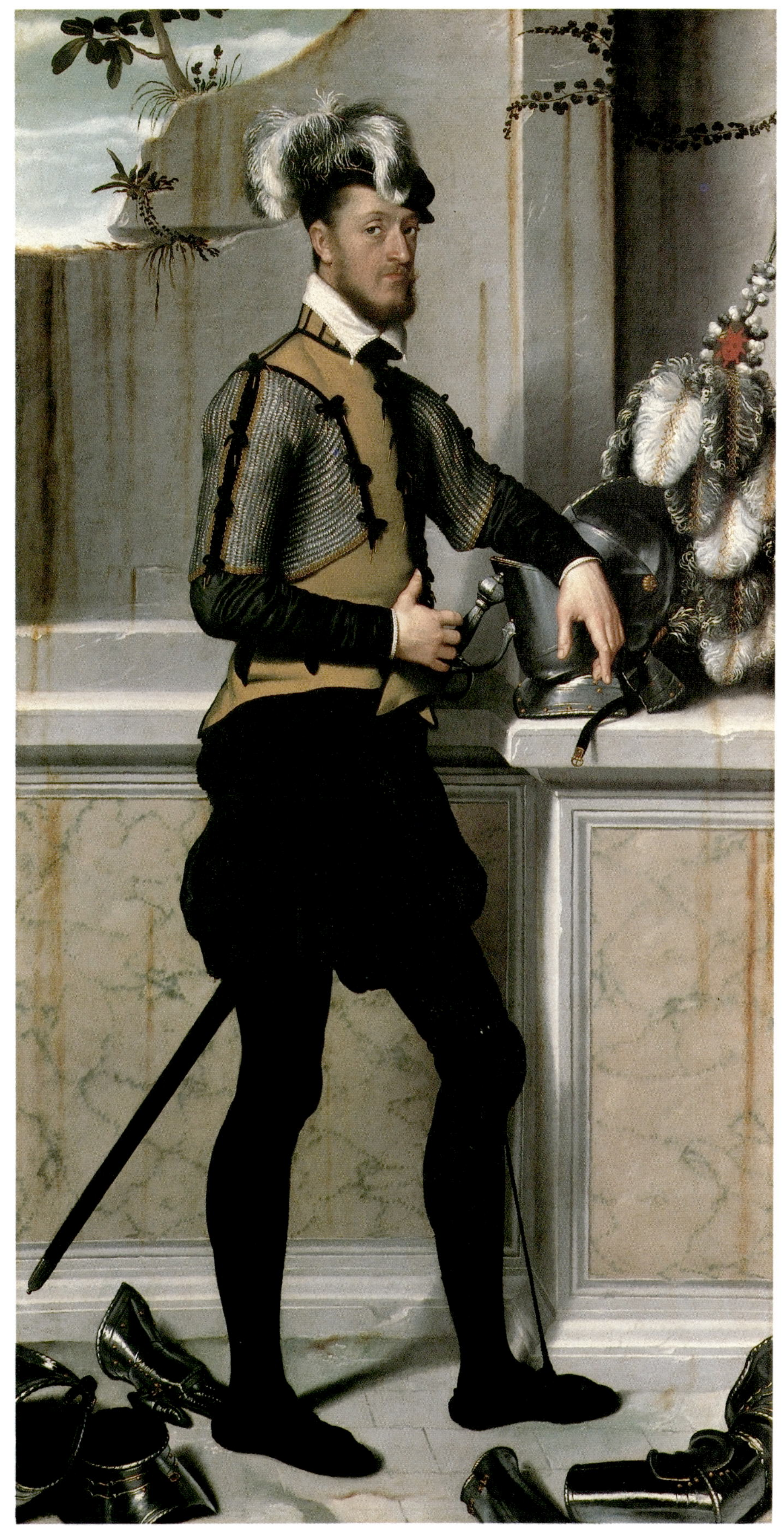

Giovan Battista Moroni, active 1546/7; died 1578

Portrait of a Man ('The Tailor') (No. 697)

Canvas, 97 × 74 cm.
Purchased 1862

A 'glorious portrait of a tailor by Moretto [*sic*]. It is a celebrated picture, called the "Taglia Panni". The tailor, a bright-looking man with a ruff, has his shears in his beautifully painted hands, and is looking at the spectator. It will be a popular picture.' Thus Lady Eastlake described Moroni's '*The Tailor*', which had just been purchased by her husband for the National Gallery, the first of no less than ten portraits by the painter that were eventually to enter the collection. Since the seventeenth century, when in the Palazzo Grimani at Venice, this had been the most famous of Moroni's portraits, the painting that almost alone ensured that the reputation of the painter was not entirely submerged in the centuries following his death. The reasons for its popularity are not difficult to discover, for what is exceptional about the portrait, and what remained exceptional even in the nineteenth century, is that it should show not a gentleman, but an artisan – pictured with natural dignity and actually engaged in his trade.

Even today there are those who find it difficult to credit that the sitter was indeed a tailor, and who argue that he may rather be a cloth merchant. However this may be, it is not uncharacteristic of Moroni's impartial approach to portraiture that his most famous masterpiece should be such a picture, carried out at a time, probably in the later 1560s, that witnessed the early emergence of the professions and the consequent decline of the feudal aristocracy. Social considerations are not without their relevance to the painting as a work of art, for the sitter is distinguished even in the colours he wears from the more fashionable clients of Moroni's later years. Just as Moroni increasingly emphasized the angularity of the human body in his portraits, so more tightly fitting clothes of black replaced the looser and more colourful garments of the earlier sixteenth century. The red breeches of the tailor are contrasted with the black material, marked with white lines in chalk, which is before him on the table.

The light falls from the left across the painting, creating pockets of dark shadow on the buff jacket of the tailor. In silhouette the pose is more substantial than usual in Moroni's works, the left arm stretched out to facilitate the cutting of the cloth. Despite the pyramidal cast of the composition, the head is inclined downwards towards the work-table, while the eyes look directly from the painting – a professional appraisal that takes, almost literally, the measure of the spectator.

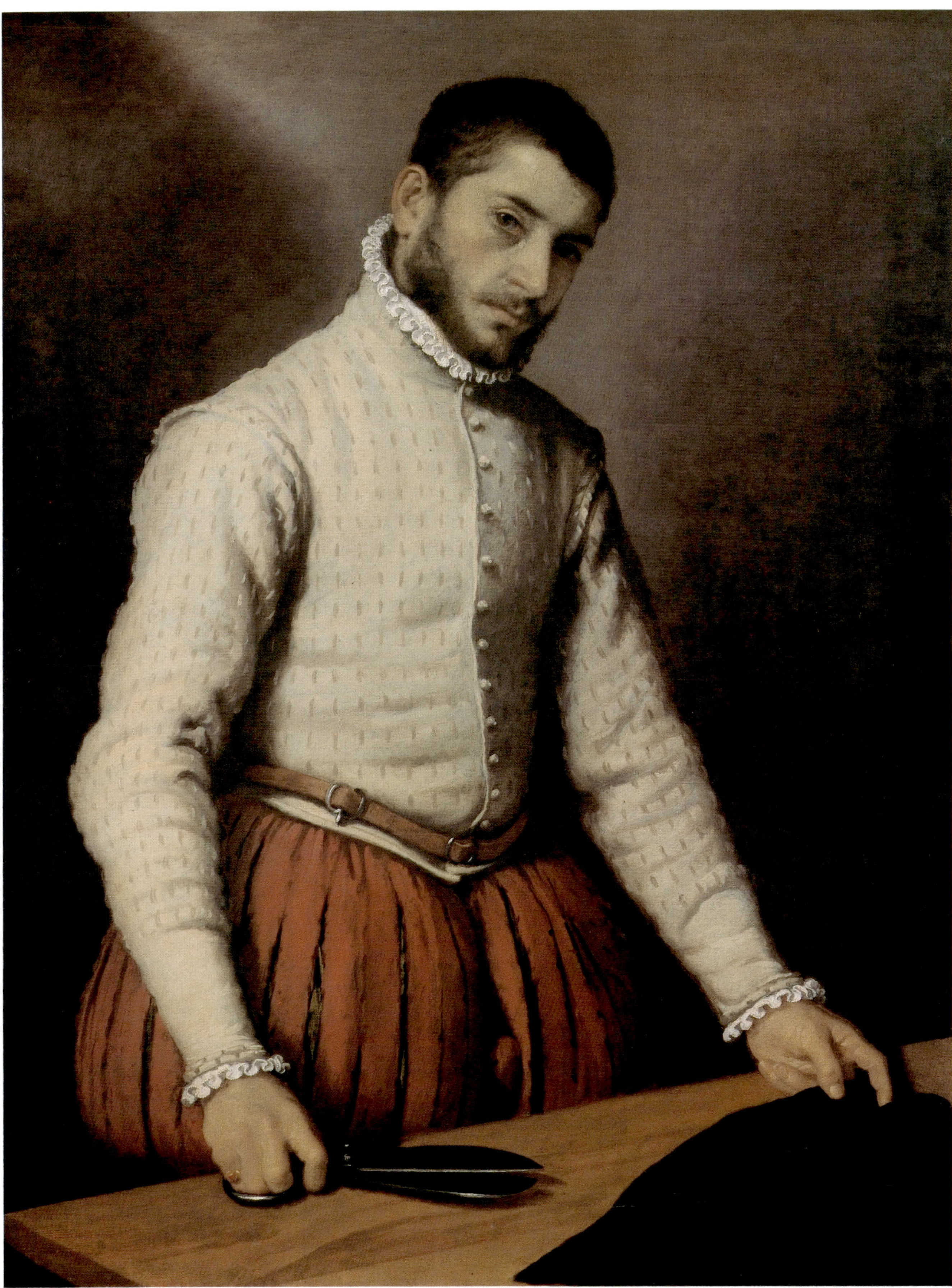

Index to Plates

Note : page numbers throughout refer to the position of the illustrations